THE BEST FREE
HISTORIC ATTRACTIONS
IN OREGON & WASHINGTON

Favorite Freebies Volume 1

1890 Steam Donkey - Pacific County Historical Museum

THE BEST FREE
HISTORIC ATTRACTIONS
IN OREGON & WASHINGTON

Favorite Freebies Volume 1

By KiKi Canniff

Ki2 Enterprises
P.O. Box 13322
Portland, Oregon

Library of Congress Cataloging-in-Publication Data

Canniff, KiKi
The best free historic attractions in Oregon & Washington / by KiKi
Canniff
p.   cm. — (Favorite freebies: vol. 1)
Includes index.
ISBN 0-941361-01-2 : $10.95
1. Oregon - Guidebooks.   2. Washington (State) - Guidebooks.   3.
Historic sites - Oregon - Guidebooks.   4. Historic sites - Washington
(State) - Guidebooks.
I. Title.   II. Series: Canniff, KiKi - Favorite freebies: vol. 1.
F874.3.C34   1992
917.9504'43—dc20   92-14405   CIP

ISBN# 0-941361-01-2

Ki^2 Enterprises
P.O. Box 13322
Portland, Oregon 97213

Dedicated to Mom and Dad
who gifted me with the spirit of adventure
and John who encourages me to let it soar.

TABLE OF CONTENTS

Antique car collection - Lynden Pioneer Museum

INTRODUCTION

I'm an explorer. If I'd been around 500 years ago, you would have found me sailing the oceans, charting new lands. Or 200 years ago, pioneering North America's western territories. But being born midway in the twentieth century, I travel for fun. I'm just as serious as those early adventurers, and I gather information to share with others. I gather that information for you, my readers, so that you can enjoy the best of Oregon and Washington.

I was raised by adventurous parents. They packed us up and moved west in the 1950s. My memories of this first journey are of a time when campgrounds were rare and we were among the few who visited some of America's finest places; places I've revisited as an adult that have since become popular tourist attractions. Later that decade we made another journey in a school bus Dad converted for family travel. That was long before bus conversions were popular; RVs and travel trailers were rare.

I've never forgotten those days. In fact, it taught me about the bonds a family forms when they share adventures. As I later explored this region on my own, I shared those joys with my own daughter. She grew up learning to read on road signs and learned history in museums and at the sights where history took place. She learned geography the same way I did, first hand. It gave her a head start on her classmates and warm memories that she'll carry through life.

As I made my way across Oregon and Washington, I took particular pleasure in getting away from the main roads. I did this with no purpose in mind except seeing where those other roads would lead. I stopped to meet the people who lived off the beaten path, visit their favorite haunts and taste the flavor of the region. Over the years I've visited nearly 4,000 recreational attractions and camped in every National Forest in the two states. In the process, I found 3,000 free attractions and nearly 2,000 public campgrounds.

My first guides to the area's free attractions began appearing in 1982. *Oregon Free* and *Washington Free* catalogued everything a family could do for free. Over the years I have found it difficult to maintain the accuracy of those first editions. I didn't want to visit the same attractions every year or two and could not bear the thought of presenting my readers with out of date information. Explorers are not too keen about repeating the same old trips and I had other books I needed to write. Consequently those two titles are now out of print.

Lots of readers have asked me which attractions I enjoyed the most, and I definitely have some favorites. This new series was designed to fill the gap those first two best selling volumes have left behind. It will take you to see my favorite freebies. This first volume, *The Best Free Historic Attractions in Oregon & Washington*, is a great way to explore the region's early beginnings. Other books in the series will show you where to find the best free places to take your kids, coastal freebies, and the best of the region's scenic places. If you'd like to be on a mailing list so you'll know when new volumes are out, send your name and address, to my attention, care of Ki^2 Books.

This book is designed for easy use. Each state has its own section, each place within that state its own number. In the front of each section you'll find a map. To get the most out of this book, read it in its entirety and mark those attractions that you find most intriguing; then refer to the map for nearby attractions and those places located between where you are and the sights you'd most like to visit. This method is sure to give you plenty to see along the way. The towns I've included on my locator maps are all listed on the states' official highway maps. I recommend that you use those maps to plot your drive; use the book's maps to plan your visit.

If you enjoy camping, you'll find the region's hundreds of free campgrounds detailed in *Free Campgrounds of Washington & Oregon.* Those of you who want showers and other civilized facilities are better off with *A Camper's Guide to Oregon & Washington.* It details the "pay" campgrounds. These two campground guides have the distinction of being the only ones written by a Northwest resident and contain hundreds of campgrounds missed by other guides.

KiKi Canniff
Author

Special Note: Although the museums listed in this book are all free, they rely on volunteer help and donations to keep the doors open.

OREGON'S BEST FREE
HISTORIC ATTRACTIONS

OREGON MAP

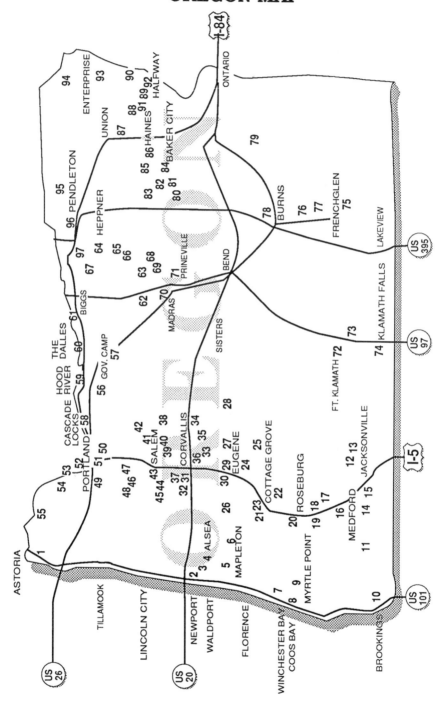

OREGON

1863 Civil War Fort

1 ♦ The **Fort Stevens Historical Area** is very special and a favorite with military buffs. It was the base of military operations from 1865 to 1947. The fort was first constructed during the Civil War allowing Union solders to protect the Columbia River from Confederate invasion.

The best way to see the old fort is to take the walking tour that begins near the visitor's center. It will lead you through the remains of buildings and batteries. Tour highlights include a torpedo loading room, eight concrete gun batteries and the mine loading building. You can also visit Battery Russell's fire control tower.

Underground cannon room - Fort Stevens

The original fort was earthwork, a fort built mainly of dirt, and included several buildings. To protect the fort from land attack it was surrounded by a moat, complete with drawbridge. This Civil War fort was equipped with smoothbore Parrott rifles and Rodman cannons that required 14 men for firing.

In 1897 eight concrete gun batteries were added. Each was armed with a 10" cannon plus long and short range rifles. Battery Russell was built around 1904 and held 12" mortars and 10" disappearing rifles. A control tower was necessary to direct the firing of the battery's big guns.

During World War II Fort Stevens housed 2,500 soldiers. New barracks had to be built and another gun battery was added. This one held two 6" rifles with a 15 mile range, almost double that of the 10" rifles.

2nd U.S. Artillery - Fort Stevens

Throughout the summer fort visitors can watch living history demonstrations featuring costumed Civil War soldiers. If your timing is right you might also see unusual military vehicles or vintage autos and trucks.

This historic area includes a Military Museum housed in the former World War II War Games Command Center where you can view artifacts dating from the Civil War. During the summer you can also take a guided tour of the underground Battery Mishler or ride in a 1954 Army truck for a tour of the 37 acre historical area. These guided tours and the museum are not free.

Fort Stevens is located in Hammond, 10 miles west of Astoria. Exhibits are open daily throughout the summer, 10 am to 6 pm. Winter hours are 10 am to 4 pm weekdays only.

Beaded Indian Skirts and Pioneer Pets

2♦ Don't let anyone ever tell you museums are all the same. I've visited every museum in the Pacific Northwest and they're all different. At the **Burrows House**, in Newport, we found a wonderful exhibit honoring pioneer pets. It was my daughter's favorite. I really enjoyed the 1860s photos of Newport as a popular seaside resort and learning about the hardships those first vacationers were willing to endure to get there. The Burrows House is filled with furniture, clothing and housewares used by coastal settlers. Another special item is an early electric stove that would dwarf most modern-day kitchens. This

1895 house served as a boarding house in its early years and later as a funeral parlor.

Next door, in the **Log Cabin Museum**, you'll find an outstanding collection of Siletz Indian artifacts. I've never seen so many well preserved Indian beaded skirts in one display. You can also see maritime, farming and logging tools, an early jigsaw and a ship captain's desk that is over 200 years old.

This terrific pair of museums is located in Newport at 545 and 579 S.W. Ninth Street. They are open Tuesday thru Sunday. Summer hours are 10 am to 5 pm, winter hours 11 am to 4 pm.

Five Coastal Area Covered Bridges

At one time Oregon had more than 450 covered bridges. They dotted the countryside; wooden, barn-like sentinels spanning rivers, streams and creeks. They were designed to extend the life of wooden bridges in our rainy environment. Most have disappeared, but some of my favorites still stand just a short ride from the Oregon coast.

3♦ You'll find two bridges east of Waldport. The first one is in the rugged foothills of Lincoln County at a picturesque spot where five streams come together. The **Fisher School Covered Bridge** is 72' long and was built in 1919. The framing logs were cut and shaped with broadaxes. To view this bridge, leave Waldport on State Highway 34 heading east. After 20 miles take Five Rivers Road to the right and follow it for about 9 miles, bearing left at Siletz Road. The bridge is on the right and only open to foot traffic.

4 ♦ Hayden Covered Bridge, one of the state's oldest, is found 28 miles east of Waldport, just off State Highway 34. Built in 1918, this 91' beauty spans the Alsea River two miles west of Alsea. It is located just south of the highway on Hayden Road.

5 ♦ You'll find the other three bridges northeast of Florence. Head east 12 miles on State Highway 126 to the town of Mapleton. The first two bridges are northwest of town. Take State Highway 36 north 13 miles to the town of Deadwood. To view the **Deadwood Creek Covered Bridge** follow Deadwood Creek Road north 5 miles. This 105' bridge was built in 1932. To find the **Lake Creek Covered Bridge** follow State Highway 36 an additional 4 miles past Deadwood to its junction with Nelson Mountain Road. Heading east, you'll find the bridge .5 mile down this road. Built in 1928, the 105' bridge spans Lake Creek.

6 ♦ To view the third bridge take State Highway 126 east of Mapleton 9 miles. At Stagecoach Road head north to **Wildcat Covered Bridge**. This 75' bridge was built over Wildcat Creek in 1925.

1892 Lighthouse

7 ♦ In 1855 the mouth of the Umpqua River was chosen as the sight of the Oregon Territory's first lighthouse. That first structure was destroyed by floods in 1861. The second **Umpqua River Lighthouse** was built on firmer ground. Completed in 1892, its 67' conical tower rises 165' above sea level. It is fitted with a 4,000 pound hollow lens containing 1,000 hand cut prisms. The lense revolves around a stationary lamp which produces a 210,000 candlepower beam that can be seen for 19 miles.

You'll find Umpqua River Lighthouse 1.5 miles south of Winchester Bay. Just past the lighthouse is a former U.S. Coast Guard Station that now houses the **Douglas County Coastal Historical Center**. Inside, you can learn all about the lighthouse, as well as early coastal shipping and timber activities. The center is open May thru September from 10 am to 5 pm Wednesday thru Saturday and 1 to 5 pm on Sundays.

A Tribute to the Lost Art of Hand Set Printing

8♦ The printed page is something we all take for granted. Books, magazines, newspapers, newsletters, birthday cards and even restaurant menus are mass produced. At the **Marshfield Sun Printing Museum** in Coos Bay you can see how printing was done before the industry was controlled by computers. As a former typesetter and a desk top publishing enthusiast, I really enjoyed this opportunity to show my daughter how the industry has changed!

Much of the equipment housed here was used to print the town's first newspaper. The Marshfield Sun was established in 1891, when Coos Bay was still called Marshfield. The paper was set and printed by hand until 1944. You can rediscover this rapidly disappearing art between 1 and 4 pm, Tuesday thru Saturday, during the summer months. At other times you'll need to call (503) 756-6156 for an appointment. You'll find the museum on US Highway 101 at Front Street, in downtown Coos Bay.

Butt Rigging, Pickaroons and Whistlepunks

9 ♦ You'll learn all about those colorful expressions and plenty of others at the **Coos County Logging Museum** in Myrtle Point. Established as a tribute to old-time logging, this museum contains everything a turn-of-the-century logging camp would need. The displays are arranged by department so you'll get the feel of an actual camp.

You'll find old saws, undercutters, axes, cookhouse crockery, harnesses and yokes used with oxen and horses, stump pullers, early power saws and lots more. The museum walls are lined with photographs of old-time logging camps and operations. Logging is an important part of the area's history and you'll learn a lot about its beginnings at this museum.

The museum is located at the corner of Seventh and Maple Streets, in Myrtle Point. Housed in a 1910 round building, it is open from 10 am to 4 pm. Monday thru Saturday and between 1 and 4 pm on Sundays.

Stagecoach Way Station

10 ♦ Long before the town of Brookings was established, the old Blake House served as a stagecoach way station. Travelers making their way along the southern Oregon coast found it a welcome refuge. Visit today and you'll find the upstairs rooms furnished much as they were for those early visitors. Built in 1857, today it serves as the **Chetco Valley Historical Society Museum**.

The beautiful handmade quilts on the upstairs beds and throughout the museum are a favorite with visitors. They are in excellent condition and some date back to the Civil War. You'll also find baskets woven by the Chetco Indians, a large collection of vintage cameras, pioneer clothing, World War I souvenirs and lots of historic photos.

The museum is located at 15641 Museum Road, in Brookings. Summer hours are 12 to 5 pm Wednesday thru Sunday, the balance of the year it is open 12 to 4 pm Thursday thru Sunday. Next to the museum you can see the world's largest Monterey Cypress tree. Nicknamed **"King Monty"** by local citizens, it measures 32.5' in circumference and is between 350 and 400 years old. A short flight of stairs leads to the tree.

A Town Founded because of a Pool Table

11♦ Kerby has one of the most unusual beginnings of any town in the Pacific Northwest. It happened in the mid-1800s when Oregon's southwest corner was inhabited by gold seeking adventurers and those who made it their job to bring in whatever the miners needed. Supplies were brought up from Crescent City. One mule train carried a pool table destined for an established camp. The weight was too much for the animal to bear and it keeled over in the night. Not wanting to reload, or loose another mule, the pool hall was set up on the spot. Thus the town of Kerby was established.

You can learn about Kerby's beginnings at the **Josephine County Kerbyville Museum** which is housed in a picturesque 1860s home. Displays include historic artifacts, equipment representing 100 years of gold mining, a turn-of-the-century log school house and a reconstructed blacksmith's shop. The museum is open from May 15 thru September 15. Sunday hours are 1 to 5 pm; the rest of the week they are open from 10 am to 5 pm.

Three Southern Oregon Covered Bridges

12♦ The Medford area has three beautiful covered bridges. The first two are northeast of town; the third southwest. Head northeast on State Highway 62; after 6 miles it will join State Highway 140. Follow this road east 5 miles to Antelope Road. The 58' **Antelope Creek Covered Bridge** is 1 mile down this road, over Antelope Creek. It was built in 1922.

13♦ The **Lost Creek Covered Bridge**, at a mere 39', is Jackson County's shortest covered bridge. It was built in 1919. To find it, take State Highway 140 an additional 9 miles east of Antelope Road to the Lake Creek Exit. From there, follow South Fork Little Butte Road to Lost Creek Road. The bridge is .5 mile south.

14♦ To find the third bridge leave Medford on State Highway 238. At Ruch, 13 miles southwest of town, turn south on Applegate Road. You will find the 122' **McKee Covered Bridge** along the Applegate River, 8 miles south of Ruch. Built in 1917, this picturesque spot offers picnic facilities and a swimming hole.

A Gold Rush Town that Never Died

15 ♦ The entire town of Jacksonville has been declared a **National Historic Landmark**. Established in 1851, it was built around the site of the region's first gold discovery. Reminders of the town's colorful beginnings have been carefully preserved. The best place to start your tour is at the marker on Applegate and Oak where those first gold nuggets were found.

In downtown **Jacksonville** you can walk down streets lined with wooden and brick buildings that look just like they did during the gold rush. Jacksonville has

Beekman Bank

never been a ghost town. After the gold rush ended it evolved into a prosperous agricultural center. It remains a living and working reminder of the nineteenth century. The oldest surviving brick building is at Oregon and Main Streets. It was built in 1855. A free brochure pointing out **86 historic buildings** is available around town.

Be sure to visit the old **Jacksonville Cemetery**. It was first used in 1859. Many of the town's pioneers are buried here along with a lot of men and women lured by gold fever. The sexton's tool house was built with a trap door in the floor where bodies were stored until graves could be prepared. The cemetery's hilltop location also provides an excellent view of the surrounding area which is peppered with lovely Victorian homes.

Shortly after gold was discovered here in 1851, Jacksonville became the center of the region's gold rush activities. The **Beekman Bank** had more than $30 million in gold passed over its counters. The bank has been preserved much as it was during the gold rush. They have installed large viewing windows where visitors will see exhibits relating Jacksonville's golden history. The town also has a wonderful historical museum and some lovely old homes that are open for touring but they are not free.

A Gem of a Rock Museum

16 ♦ Fossils, petrified woods, stone Indian artifacts, geodes, minerals, rock carvings and a huge crystal collection are among the items found at the **Crater**

Rock Museum. Kids of all ages find rock collecting an inexpensive yet exciting hobby and this museum is a great place to expand or encourage those interests.

Oregon is a rockhound's paradise. This Central Point museum is a terrific place to learn what rocks are found in Oregon and where to look. Their lighted showcases will keep an avid rock hound busy for hours. My family particularly enjoyed the Rogue River Indian arrowheads, gold nuggets and the expansive collection of crystals and agatized stones.

Rain or shine, this is a terrific place to spend some time. From I-5 take exit #35 at Central Point and follow State Highway 99 a short distance to Scenic Avenue. Turn left to 2002 Scenic Avenue. The museum is open Tuesday, Thursday and Saturday from 10 am to 4 pm. Each spring the people who operate the museum host a wonderful gem and mineral show. There is a small fee to attend this show.

1872 Water-powered Grist Mill

17♦ On the banks of Little Butte Creek you can visit one of America's few remaining water-powered grist mills. The **Butte Creek Mill** was built in 1872. As you step inside the cool interior you are greeted by the soft, rhythmic sound of water as it turns the 1400 pound millstones of this thriving operation.

Visitors can watch the miller work the grain just as previous millers have for over a hundred years. The mammoth round millstones were quarried in France, assembled in Illinois, shipped around Cape Horn to Crescent City, then carried over the mountains by wagon to Eagle Point. Downstairs you can see the belts, shafts and pulleys that move the stones and watch as creek water runs through the millrace activating the turbine that turns the wheels.

This rustic old building is listed on the National Register of Historic Places. The foundation pillars are two feet square and were hewn with a broad axe. Its beams are morticed together and pinned with hard wooden pegs. The walls are made of whipsawed lumber and fastened with square nails. To get there from I-5, take exit #30 and follow State Highway 62 north 10 miles. The address is 402 Royal Avenue North. Visitors are welcome Monday thru Saturday between 9 am and 5 pm.

A Pioneer Burial Marked by a Covered Bridge

18♦ The 1846 burial of a pioneer child gave Grave Creek its name. Traveling with her family from Missouri, Martha Leland Crowley died there beside the creek and was buried beneath a prominent oak tree. During the Indian wars of the 1850s, a fort was established next to the creek and named Fort Leland in her honor.

In 1921 the **Sunny Valley Covered Bridge** was built across Grave Creek. It sits just east of I-5, at the Sunny Valley exit. The picturesque 105' bridge is so close to the freeway that no history buff, no matter how much of a hurry they're in, can find an excuse for passing it by.

Turn-of-the-century Miner's Cabin

19♦ Whiskey Creek Cabin is the oldest known, still-standing, miner's cabin in the remote lower Rogue River Canyon. The cabin consists of a main house, pantry, blacksmith shop, generator shed, solar shower, tool shed and outhouse. Water runs by gravity thru a pipeline to an outside tap. The solar-heated shower, fir floor and sawdust insulated pantry were not part of the original construction. Visitors can't go inside but can look thru the windows and wander around the site. The flume ditch near the cabin was dug around 1890. It begins .5 mile up Whiskey Creek and ends at the gully, just behind the tool shed.

To find the cabin, leave I-5 at the Sunny Valley exit and head west. Take the Mt. Reuben-Whiskey Creek Access Road. You will have to hike the last .7 mile along a steep dirt road. The cabin is located along the Rogue River, three miles downstream from Grave Creek, just off the Rogue River Trail.

Six Million Years of Natural History

20♦ One of Southern Oregon's finest museums offers the opportunity to learn about everything from saber-toothed cats to how humans lived 8,000 years ago. At the **Douglas County Museum of History and Natural History** the natural history exhibits begin with 6-million-year-old prehistoric mammals and end with current species like Oregon's black bear.

Native American exhibits include tools used thousands of years ago, prior to the exploding of Mt.

Mazama and the creation of Crater Lake. You'll learn about the hardships pioneers endured as they traveled to their new homes, see pioneer logging equipment and agricultural tools and discover how the Northwest fur industry operated.

Four wings of exhibits make this an entertaining stop for everyone. You'll find the museum near Umpqua Park, in Roseburg. From I-5 take exit #123 one mile south of town. The museum is open Tuesday thru Saturday from 10 am to 4 pm and Sunday from 12 to 4 pm.

The Golden Past of Cottage Grove

The foothills southeast of Cottage Grove have a rich history; one that was shaped by gold rush fever. The Bohemia Mining District was one of the richest spots in the Cascade Mountains. Gold was first found along Sharp's Creek in 1858 and the rush that followed resulted in millions of dollars worth of gold being taken from the area.

21♦ Before driving out to the old mining area stop at the **Cottage Grove Historical Museum** for a look at what life was like during the gold rush. You'll find antique mining equipment as well as an actual working model of an 1870 stampmill. Other museum exhibits include Indian artifacts, a working model of an 1860 water-powered sawmill plus lots of pioneer tools and furnishings. The museum is housed in an 1897 octagonal church building that includes some beautiful Italian stained glass windows. You can visit the museum between 1 and 4 pm. During the summer

Stampmill - Cottage Grove Historical Museum

they are open Wednesday thru Sunday; the balance of the year they are only open on weekends. It is located at "H" and Birch Avenues.

22 ♦ To find the **Bohemia Mining District**, leave town on Row River Road; from I-5 it's the Dorena exit. After 17 miles, at Culp Creek, head south on Sharp's Creek Road. The road is rough and steep but after about 16 miles, near the top of Bohemia Mountain, you will find a few of the old buildings. The view from the mountain top is spectacular. Gold is still found in this area and actively mined along Sharp's Creek.

The Covered Bridge Capital of Oregon

There are 18 covered bridges still standing in Lane County. The Cottage Grove and Eugene areas have 15 of those historic bridges. Among them you will find the only remaining covered railroad bridge as well as the state's longest covered bridge.

23 ♦ In and around Cottage Grove you can visit five covered bridges. The **Chambers Covered Railroad Bridge** was built in 1936 so trains could bring logs right into the Frank Chambers Mill. It crosses the Coast Fork of the Willamette River. The construction includes steel reinforcing rods necessary to support the moving weight of the heavily loaded railroad cars. The tall portals were also an important design feature as the timber was stacked quite high. This 78' bridge was last used by trains in the late 1950s. To find the bridge, simply follow State Highway 99 into Cottage Grove until you reach Main Street. Head west thru town and turn on South River Road.

The other four local covered bridges are reached via Row River Road, east of Cottage Grove. The **Mosby Creek Covered Bridge** is the oldest in Lane County and is still open to motor vehicles. It was built in 1920. This 90' span is supported by wooden pilings and has steel rod cross-braces on the upper chords.

Mosby Creek Covered Bridge

To find the bridge, head east out of Cottage Grove 2 miles to Row River Road and then south to Mosby Creek Road. Drive southwest on this road for 2 miles to Layng Road and the bridge.

The **Stewart Covered Bridge** is .5 mile further along Mosby Creek Road. Constructed of douglas fir, it also crosses Mosby Creek. The bridge was built in 1930 and utilizes the Howe Truss. This 60' bridge has no viewing windows but is ventilated through slits near the roof.

The colorful **Currin Covered Bridge** sports barn red side walls and white entrance portals. Its corrugated metal roof protects hand-hewn chords. You'll find the bridge east of Cottage Grove, 4 miles along Row River Road. Built in 1925, this 105' span crosses Row River. The 105' **Star/Dorena Covered Bridge** also spans the Row River. Constructed in 1949, you'll find it near Dorena. From the Currin bridge, head east 1 mile on Row River Road then turn on Government Road for an additional 7 miles. The bridge features spliced Howe Trusses, eave windows and wooden shingles.

24 ◆ You'll find another four covered bridges southeast of Eugene. To view the **Parvin Covered Bridge** follow State Highway 58 southeast 13 miles to the town of Dexter. From there, take Parvin Road to Lost Creek. Although traffic now bypasses it, this 1921 bridge was once the scene of much activity.

The town of Lowell is reached by taking State Highway 58 for an additional two miles turning north on Lowell Road. There you will find the 1945 **Lowell Covered Bridge** straddling the Middle Fork of the Willamette River. It is 165' long. The **Unity Covered Bridge** is just a short distance north of Lowell. Go through town and take Unity Place Road. This bridge straddles Big Fall Creek. Built in 1936, it is 90' long. The **Pengra Covered Bridge** is northwest of Unity. Follow Place Road west to its junction with Little Fall Creek Road where you will find the 120' bridge spanning Fall Creek. It was built in 1938.

25 ♦ Back at Dexter you can take State Highway 58 southeast 23 miles for a look at Oregon's longest covered bridge. Another interesting feature on the **Office Covered Bridge** is its separate covered walkway. You will find this bridge in the town of Westfir, just north of Oakridge. The 180' bridge was built in 1944.

26 ♦ To find the **Coyote Creek Covered Bridge** follow State Highway 126 west of Eugene to the town of Veneta. Turn south on Territorial Highway and follow this to Battle Creek Road. The 60' Coyote Creek bridge was built in 1922.

27 ♦ East of Eugene, State Highway 126 will lead you to four more covered bridges. The **Goodpasture Covered Bridge** sits near a bend in the McKenzie River and is probably the most-photographed bridge in Oregon. To reach it, simply take State Highway 126 northeast for 23 miles to the town of Vida. The bridge was built in 1938 and is 165' long. You'll find plenty of parking areas along the highway where you can safely park while you take your own photograph.

28 ♦ The 120' **Belknap Covered Bridge** also straddles the McKenzie River. It was built in 1966. To reach it from Vida, continue east on State Highway 126 an additional 30 miles. Turn south just before you reach the town of McKenzie Bridge, onto McKenzie River Drive. From here it is 2.2 miles to the bridge.

29 ♦ You'll find the last two bridges in Marcola, a small town 14 miles northeast of Springfield. To get to Marcola follow 14th Street east out of town. This soon becomes Marcola Road and after an additional 7 miles you arrive in Marcola. At the northeast end of town turn right on Wendling Road for 1.7 miles, then turn left onto Pachelke Road. The **Ernest Covered Bridge** is 1.3 miles further. This bridge was built in 1938 and spans the Mohawk River. To find the **Wendling Covered Bridge**, you would also head east on Wendling Road. The bridge is situated 3.5 miles from town, on Wendling Road, over Mill Creek. Built in 1938, it is 60' long.

Wendling Covered Bridge

Oregon's Finest Fossil Collection

30 ♦ The **University of Oregon Museum of Natural History** in Eugene is packed with outstanding exhibits. Among the museum's best features is a fossil collection that has long been one of the largest in the U.S. It includes specimens gathered by Thomas Condon during his discovery of the John Day Fossil Beds in the 1860s. Its value exceeds $5 million.

The museum is also custodian to all state-secured anthropological and archaeological materials. Their anthropology collection was established in 1935 and contains many unique specimens. At the museum's herbarium you will find displays that include a large number of plant specimens gathered around the turn of the century. The zoology department features bird nests, eggs and plenty of mounted specimens. Museum hours are 12 to 5 pm Wednesday thru Saturday.

When the University of Oregon first opened in 1876, it was situated on a barren knoll in a treeless pasture. Donations made since that time have made it possible to create a campus sporting more than 400 different types of trees and a beautiful setting taking up 250 acres. A guide to campus trees is available at the museum.

You can also get a map that will take you on a self-guided tour of the campus. Visitors are welcome in all of the buildings. If you're short on time, at least visit **Deadly Hall**. Built in 1876, this was the school's first building. In fact, it was the only building for the first ten years. It is located in the northwest corner of the campus. Nearby, in Allen Hall you can see the hand press that was used to print the first newspaper west of the Mississippi. The free map will help you to find a number of handsome sculptures and interesting displays that exist on campus.

The University of Oregon campus is also home to a wonderful **Museum of Art**. This is the only state supported art museum in Oregon and features extensive collections of both Northwest and Oriental art. They also have a large collection of African craft pieces; Ghana and Nigeria are particularly well represented. Architects will particularly enjoy the photographs of buildings throughout the nation designed by internationally famous Northwest architect Pietro Beluschi. The museum also houses more than 500 works by Morris Graves. They are open 12 to 5 pm Wednesday thru Sunday. There is sometimes a charge for special exhibits. This building is adjacent to the library.

Oregon's Oldest Museum & Slices of History

31♦ Until 1851 Benton County included all of the lands between the Pacific Ocean and the Willamette River, from California to Kings Valley. Today it is one of the state's smallest counties. The county seat, Corvallis, has a number of beautiful old buildings. Stop at the Corvallis Convention & Visitors Bureau for detailed maps and information on their locations.

The **1888 Benton County Courthouse**, in Corvallis, is the oldest courthouse in Oregon still used for its original purpose. This handsome stone and brick building retains many of its original features. Italianate in design, this elegant building sports a low flat roof, overhanging eaves, tall windows and a clock tower. The original clock mechanism, purchased in 1888, still operates the clock today. A statue of Themis, the Greek Goddess of Justice, stands guard

Benton County Courthouse

over the east entrance just as she has since the beginning. Inside you will find some of the original furniture still in use. They include the first judge's bench, jury box, spectator benches, library table and coat rack. Visitors are welcome during normal business hours. The address is 120 N.W. Fourth Street.

At the **Horner Museum**, on the Oregon State University campus, you will find an outstanding collection of items representing the region's rich cultural and scientific heritage. The museum got its start prior to 1868 when the university was still known as Corvallis College.

This is the oldest museum in Oregon. Exhibits include a prehistoric mastodon tusk, Victorian furniture, ancient Chinese coins, embroidered wall hangings, Native American artifacts, fossils and natural history displays. Visitors can experience history from prehistoric time to the present. It's a treasure chest that will teach you a lot about Oregon Country settlers. Throughout the school year the museum is also open Tuesday thru Friday from 10 am to 5 pm, Saturday 12 to 4 pm and Sunday 12 to 5 pm. Summer hours are 10 am to 5 pm Monday thru Friday and 12 to 5 pm on Sundays.

Six miles west of Corvallis, in Philomath, the **Benton County Historical Museum** is another terrific place to learn about the area's history. Displays include a priceless collection of quilts, coverlets and fabrics plus pioneer musical instruments, toys and furnishings. You can visit an early newspaper office filled with antique typesetting and printing equipment and look

Benton County Historical Museum

at lots of historic photographs. You'll also learn about the role logging and agriculture played in the county's beginnings and the tragic tale of the area's first residents, the Kalapuya Indians. The museum is located at 1101 Main Street. Hours are 10 am to 4:30 pm Tuesday thru Saturday.

Corvallis Area Covered Bridges

32 ♦ The Corvallis area has three historic covered bridges just a short distance from I-5. The first is located west of the city, near Wren. The aging **Harris Covered Bridge** was built in 1936 and spans Marys River. From Corvallis, take State Highway 20 to Wren and head west 2.5 miles on Harris Road to the bridge.

33 ♦ The **Crawfordsville Covered Bridge** is southeast of Corvallis. Follow I-5 south 12 miles to

State Highway 228 and go east 11 miles to Crawfordsville. The 105' bridge crosses the Calapooya River. Built in 1932, it was bypassed by State Highway 228 in 1963. A county park has been built around the bridge to commemorate its historic significance.

Harris Covered Bridge

34 ◆ To view the third covered bridge, leave Crawfordsville and follow State Highway 228 east and north to State Highway 20. Take this highway east 14 miles to Cascadia and the **Short Covered Bridge**. The first covered bridge was built at this location in 1845. This is the last of the covered bridges to span the South Fork of the Santiam River. It's open sided style and wood shingle roof give it a pleasant appearance. The present structure was built in 1945 and is 105' long. To reach it, follow High Deck Road.

Old Guns, Pioneer Artifacts and Metal Detectors

35 ♦ If you like playing around with a metal detector, you'll get a real kick out of **White's Electronic Museum**. This is the only place I know of in the Pacific Northwest where you can explore the history of metal detectors. You'll not only get a chance to see some of the early models but also some of the items they have located. Gold nuggets and old coins are among the treasures. The museum is located in Sweet Home at 1011 Pleasant Valley Road. Hours are from 8 am to 5 pm weekdays and 9 am to 4 pm on Saturdays.

At the **East Linn Museum**, 746 Long Street, you will find thousands of pioneer artifacts. I particularly enjoyed the period rooms furnished with antique furniture and household goods. They also have a saddlery, blacksmith shop, logging tools, mining equipment and a nice rock collection. Jewelry, old bottles, antique dolls, well-used churns and a collection of old guns are other special treats at this lovely little museum. Also featured are artifacts from the Kalapuya and Santiam Indian tribes. The museum is open year round, Thursday thru Sunday, between 1 and 5 pm.

One of Oregon's Oldest Pioneer Communities

36 ♦ Brownsville's first pioneers arrived prior to 1850, so when George Colbert and John Moyer arrived in 1852 there was plenty of work for the two young carpenters. Among their early buildings was a house on Blakely Avenue for Hugh Brown, the man for whom the town was later named. In 1857 Moyer married Brown's daughter, Elizabeth.

The next 25 years brought the Moyers good fortune. They were involved in a number of local businesses including a bank, woolen mills and a sash and door factory. Needing a larger house befitting his successful position, Moyer drew up plans for an elaborate Italianate villa. He built this home with the help of his old friend George Colbert. When the **Moyer House** was finished in 1881, it included twelve-foot ceilings, a white Italian marble fireplace and curved walnut banisters. Landscapes and scenes in oil were painted on ceilings, walls and window transoms.

Moyer House

The house now belongs to the Linn County Historical Society and is undergoing restoration. The outside has been returned to its original green and cream colors. The inside is furnished with period antiques. You can visit the Moyer House on Saturday between 11 am and 4 pm or Sunday between 1 and 5 pm. You'll find it on Main Street, in Brownsville.

The **Linn County Historical Museum** is great place to learn more about Brownsville's early citizens. It is housed in the old Brownsville Depot and includes some old railroad cars. They have even turned one box car into a theater. This museum captures the essence of pioneer life. You can visit an old time barber shop, general store, bank and milliner's shop. An original pioneer wagon stands in the lobby along with a number of items brought across the plains on the Oregon Trail. The Kalapuya Indians and area wildlife are also well represented. Changing exhibits make this a museum worth revisiting. Located at 101 Park Avenue, they are open Tuesday thru Saturday, May thru September, from 11 am to 4 pm and Sundays from 1 to 5 pm . The balance of the year hours remain the same but they are only open Thursday thru Sunday.

Grand Old Town with 350 Historic Buildings

37 ♦ Albany is architecturally unique. It has the most varied collection of historic buildings in the state; no other city has more vintage homes. Visitors will discover some 350 historic buildings. Many are listed in the National Register of Historic Places. Most are either well preserved or have been faithfully restored.

Virtually all of these historic homes are private residences. Although they can only be viewed from the street, they offer an unequalled opportunity to see homes constructed in nine major styles popular between 1848 and 1930. Architectural styles include Federal, Classic Revival, Gothic Revival, Italianate, French Second Empire Baroque and Colonial Revival. Several architecturally elaborate churches and a number of commercial buildings are included. Detailed tour maps and brochures can be obtained at the Albany Chamber of Commerce or viewed at the permanent display in the Gazebo located at Eighth Avenue and Ellsworth Street.

The first settlers to the Albany area were farmers who came in the 1840s. In 1848 Walter and Thomas Monteith purchased a plot of land and laid out town lots on the east bank of the Willamette River, just below the mouth of the Calapooya River. In 1849 the Monteiths built their first frame house. It still stands at 518 Second Avenue SW.

In the **Downtown Historic District**, First & Second Avenue are lined with historic brick buildings. They date from 1866 to 1912. Note the cast iron pilasters and arched windows on some. Since this is an active business district, many of these buildings can be viewed from the inside.

The **Monteith Historic District** runs from Second thru Twelfth Avenues from Broadalbin to Washington Street. It includes homes built as early as 1849. Most of the **Hackleman Historic District**'s homes were built between 1868 and 1910.

1898 Niagara Dam

38 ♦ At Niagara Park, in Mill City, you can explore the remains of Oregon's first dam. The **Niagara Dam** was built here in 1898 by Italian stonemasons for the O'Neil Brothers' wheat and straw paper mill. Trails to the bottom provide close up observation. The park also offers a nature trail and picnic facilities.

Salem Area Covered Bridges

39 ♦ You'll find five scenic covered bridges east of I-5 between Albany and Salem. Their proximity to Portland make them a favorite with many. To view the 1939 **Larwood Covered Bridge**, leave the freeway heading east on State Highway 226. After about 10 miles, take Fish Hatchery Drive east 8 miles. You can swim, fish and picnic in the shadow of this 105' bridge. On the west bank of the river you will also find the remains of an old water wheel.

40 ♦ From the Larwood bridge, head north/ northwest on Larwood Drive until you arrive at Richardson Gap Road. If you take this road north 4 miles, crossing State Highway 226, you will soon come to the **Shimenek Covered Bridge**. It's one of the prettiest in the state and my favorite. This Thomas Creek location has had a covered bridge since 1861. The first one included a two-hole toilet built right into the foundation. This 130' red bridge is the fifth one built here. It was constructed in 1966.

Heading west on State Highway 226, you can visit two more covered bridges. Passing thru Scio, the highway heads south. After .5 mile take County Road #628 to County Road #629 and turn right. The lovely 120' **Gilkey Covered Bridge** is .5 mile. It was built in 1939. Until 1960 there were two covered bridges at this location. The other, a railroad bridge, is now gone.

Backtrack to State Highway 226 and continue south to find the **Hoffman Covered Bridge**. After 2.5 miles turn west on County Road #647 for 2 miles. This 1936 bridge has gothic-style windows and measures 90'. The entry portals have been enlarged to allow for passage of large loads.

41 ◆ The last bridge is northeast of Salem. Leave I-5 on State Highway 213 and head east 12 miles to Silverton. The 1916 **Gallon House Covered Bridge** crosses the Abiqua Creek north of here. It is Marion County's last remaining covered bridge. To find this 84' shingle-roofed bridge, take State Highway 214 north out of Silverton to Hobart Road. Go .2 mile on Hobart and turn left onto Gallon House Road. The bridge is .4 mile further.

Quaker Museum

42 ◆ In Scotts Mills, 7 miles northeast of Silverton, the local historical society has converted an old church into a museum. The **Scotts Mills Museum** illustrates the early Quaker settlement of the area and includes local artifacts, photographs and genealogical information. They are only open on the second Sunday of each month between 1 and 5 pm but it's well worth the trip.

Salem's Best Kept Archaeological Secret

43 ♦ Most Salem residents are unaware of this archaeological treasure. Oregon's capitol city shelters one of the finest small archaeological collections to be found anywhere. Located at the Western Baptist College, the **Robert S. Allen Archaeology Museum** offers some rare treats! Many of you will want to begin your visit with a look at the ancient coins which range from a 480 B.C. Greek Athena coin to a 15th century Byzantine gold coin.

Ever seen a falcon mummy? The museum's Egyptian room has one wrapped in the form of Osiris. This room also includes Natufian stone implements from 5000 B.C., artifacts found in Egyptian tombs, pre-dynastic vases and an alabaster canopic jar belonging to an 18th dynasty nobleman. Sumerian clay tablets from 3500 B.C. and pottery fragments bearing Nebuchadnezzar's official inscription are among the items found in the museum's main hall. More treats await you in the Manuscript and Palestinian rooms.

To get to the museum take the Mission Street exit off I-5 and follow the signs to the college at 500 Deer Park Drive S.E. The museum is located on the 2nd floor of the Library building. During the school year the museum is open 8 am to 10 pm Monday thru Thursday, closes at 5 pm on Fridays, and is open 10:30 am to 4:30 pm on Saturdays. When school is not in session you can visit on weekdays between 8 am and 4 pm.

Independence Heritage Museum

44 ◆ Independence was settled in 1845 and named after Independence, Missouri. At the city's **Heritage Museum** you can still feel the patriotism that led to its naming. Housed in an 1888 former church building, the museum is filled with pioneer momentos. It's a good place to learn more about Oregon's early beginnings. Located at Third and B Streets, the museum is open Wednesday thru Saturday from 1 to 5 pm.

Arctic Circle Artifact Collection

45 ◆ In Monmouth you'll find another, one of a kind museum. This one holds the west coast's most extensive collection of art and artifacts from the Arctic Circle. Everything on exhibit at the **Paul Jensen Arctic Museum** came from that area. Jewelry, tools, toys and clothing made from such varied materials as stone, driftwood, bone, ivory and sinew are all represented in this rare collection. The museum is located at 590 W. Church Street and open Tuesday thru Saturday 10 am to 4 pm.

1856 Military Blockhouse

46 ◆ In Dayton you can visit an authentic 1856 military blockhouse. This blockhouse was originally built southwest of town by a group of Willamette Valley settlers. Army troops named it **Fort Yamhill**. After the army abandoned Fort Yamhill as a military post, the blockhouse was used as a jail. In 1911 it was dismantled and rebuilt in Dayton. You will find the blockhouse at Dayton's Courthouse Square. A historical marker along State Highway 18, .5 mile north of Valley Junction, points out the location of the original fort.

Fort Yamhill blockhouse

Antique Farm Tool Museum

47♦ Farming is one of the world's most important occupations. Without it we could all starve. At the Lafayette **Farm Tool Museum** you have the opportunity to marvel at the equipment used by pioneer farmers to perform this backbreaking work. Other exhibits relate the historic events of the area. The museum is housed in a lovely 1893 church building.

You can visit the museum, Wednesday thru Sunday, between 1 and 5 pm throughout the summer. The balance of the year they are open weekends only from

1 to 4:30 pm. Lafayette is located six miles northeast of McMinnville and served as the county seat from 1846 to 1889.

A Couple of Pioneer Colleges

Oregon pioneers were very education minded. They established a number of fine schools and colleges even before the region was given statehood. Many of those early colleges are still around today. The following pioneer colleges have some stately old buildings and displays pertaining to their early heritage.

48 ♦ Linfield College in McMinnville was incorporated in 1858, one year before Oregon's statehood. In 1922 it acquired its current name. The historic campus has some lovely old buildings. The oldest still standing, **Pioneer Hall**, was built in 1882. The college observatory is the oldest in the northwest and houses an **1890s telescope**. Visitors are welcome at the observatory Monday thru Thursday from 9 am to 10 pm, Fridays from 9 am to 5 pm and Saturdays from 1 to 5 pm.

49 ♦ Pacific University in Forest Grove was originally established in 1848 as a school for orphans. Shortly thereafter it became known as Tualatin Academy and in 1854 was renamed Pacific University. The university's **College Hall** has a special place in Oregon history. It is the oldest building west of the Rocky Mountains built for educational purposes that is still used for that purpose. The hall has been preserved almost exactly as the pioneers built it. The original cupola still identifies the building as it did in 1850.

Inside, the building has seen few changes. You will pass through doorways installed by pioneer carpenters, surrounded by plain plank walls and panes of glass that were brought around Cape Horn on sailing ships. Upstairs, the **Pioneer Room** has an exhibit of Indian artifacts as well as numerous possessions belonging to the founders of the school and other Tualatin Valley pioneers. In the **Oriental Room** you will see pieces representative of many Asian cultures. The museum is open to the public on Wednesdays from 1 to 4 pm.

The West's First City

50♦ Oregon City has the distinction of being the first incorporated city west of the Rocky Mountains. It was founded in 1829 when Portland had only one house, Seattle was just an Indian village and San Francisco still a Spanish fortress.

Oregon City holds the title for many notable "west of the Rocky Mountain" firsts. These include the first long-range transmission of electricity which took place in 1889, the first hotel, first government, first newspaper, first public school, first library, first Protestant church, first mint, first water-powered industry, first Catholic Archdiocese, first Masonic lodge and first court of record, to name but a few. Mountain View Cemetery, on Broadway Avenue, contains the graves of many area pioneers.

Oregon City is a lovely place for a **historic driving tour**. A number of historic homes can be viewed from the street. Three special houses can be found on

Center Street. The one at 224 was built in 1869; 713 Center Street was built for Dr. John McLoughlin in 1864. It can be toured Tuesday thru Sunday for a small fee. At 719 Center is the pioneer home of Dr. Forbes Barclay. Today it serves as the Chamber of Commerce Visitors Center. Built in 1850, it showcases artifacts from Oregon's pre-statehood days. The public is welcome daily between 10 am and 4:30 pm.

Other historic Oregon City houses include the following. Unless otherwise noted they are private residences and can only be observed from the street. They include Jefferson Street - 308 (1881), 415 (1874), 902 (1893); McLoughlin Boulevard - 316 (1867), 402 (1862), 416 (1867), 604 (1866); Jerome Street - 215 (1858); Miller Street - 215 (1859); Fourth Avenue - 502 (1867); and Holmes Lane - 536 (1848). The house on Holmes Lane was originally known as the **Rose Farm** and served as the meeting place for the First Territorial Legislature. It can be toured on Sundays for a minimal charge.

Oregon's Largest Free Museum

51♦ The **Oregon Historical Society Museum** in Portland is a wonderful place. You'll find ever-changing displays honoring Pacific Northwest history, terrific permanent displays and a great research library here.

The museum's south wing houses a wealth of historical artifacts dating from prehistoric time to the present. Galleries in both the south and north wings are where you'll find the changing exhibits as well as important works by Oregon artists. A few of my favorite displays have included fashions popular in the 19th and 20th centuries, models of sailing ships important to Pacific Northwest history, photographic displays highlighting other cultures, Indian artifacts and cultural memorabilia.

Trompe d'oeil murals - Oregon Historical Center

The museum library is filled with maps, manuscripts, photographs, rare books and genealogical reference sources. It's a great source of historic information. The building is open Monday thru Saturday from 10 am to 4:30 pm. They occasionally offer a special display for which they charge an admission fee. The museum is located at 1230 S.W. Park Avenue, in downtown Portland.

Turn of the Century Buildings and Fountains

52 ♦ Downtown Portland has some gorgeous old fountains. After all, a city with this much rain has to have some place to display it all! The **Elk Fountain** at Fourth and Main was presented to the city in 1900 as a watering place for horses. Since the land here was once a feeding ground for elk, it's a very fitting piece.

The **Skidmore Fountain** was dedicated in 1888. The bronze fountain's maidens sit surrounded by grass, sycamores, old fashioned carriage lamps and rhododendrons. You can visit this lovely setting at SW First and Ankeny, near the Saturday Market.

Historic drinking fountains are also liberally sprinkled throughout the downtown area. These classy looking watering holes were donated by Simon Benson, an early Portland lumber baron. The first ones were installed during prohibition.

For those interested in historic buildings there are several areas around the city worth visiting. You might start downtown in the Skidmore Fountain/Old Town areas. This pioneer business section has many Victorian commercial structures built before the turn of the century. Another historic district is found between Stark and Yamhill, from the river to S.W. Third. Many early Portland business establishments were built there in the late 1800s.

The **Pioneer Courthouse and Post Office** at 555 S.W. Yamhill was built around 1870. This was the first federal office building in the Pacific Northwest. When first built, the building was thought by many to be too far from the business district; today it is Portland's central landmark. The building was extensively remodeled in the 1970s.

Old Church, 1422 S.W. 11th Avenue, is an example of "carpenter gothic". Built in 1882, it was a place of worship until the 1960s. It is now a historic landmark. Drop in any Wednesday at noon for the "sack lunch recital". You will be treated to music played on an organ brought around Cape Horn from Boston in 1883. This is Portland's oldest standing church structure on its original site.

The **Multnomah County Library** building at 801 S.W. 10th Avenue is listed in the National Register of Historic Places. Designed by Albert Doyle in 1912, the building pays homage to philosophers, poets, artists, and all those who help to put a book together. Many names are etched into the outside of the building. Inside, besides all the usual library items, you will find art, special reference collections, Oregon and Northwest historic materials plus other historical books, manuscripts and maps.

In northwest Portland you'll find lots of older Victorian homes and churches. King's and Lair Hills are two historic areas southwest of downtown; Ladd's Addition and Laurelhurst are southeast.

1856 Antebellum House

53 ♦ Twelve miles north of Portland, on Sauvie Island, you can tour a lovely 1856 Antebellum House. This island is steeped in history. It had several important Indian camps, was noted in the 1792 logbook of Captain George Vancouver, raved about in the Lewis & Clark journals and served as a dairy farm for the Hudson Bay Company. When the Donation Land Law was passed in 1850 settlers began to stake out this fertile island for themselves.

The **Bybee-Howell House** was built for one of those original Donation Land Claim holders. It has been restored and furnished as a pioneer homestead. The house is open for tours daily from May thru October, 10 am to 5 pm. You can also tour the grounds and visit a pioneer orchard. Operated by the Oregon Historical Society, donations are welcome. To find the Bybee-Howell House, take State Highway 30 north of Portland to the Sauvie Island Bridge. After crossing the bridge turn left; the house is 1 mile from the bridge.

Antique Courtroom and Museum

54 ♦ The first time I went in the Columbia County Courthouse it was to visit the museum. I found the old courtroom by accident and felt like I'd been transported in time. Reminiscent of courtroom scenes from scores of old movies; it is furnished much as it was when this stately basalt building was constructed in 1906.

The town of St. Helens was established in 1845. In those early years the town was the region's largest fresh water seaport, much larger than Portland. Its first school, 1847-48, was taught by Thomas Condon who went on to become a world-famous geologist. You can learn all about the town's early history at the **Columbia County Historical Museum**.

This quaint little museum is found on the second floor of the courthouse and includes pioneer artifacts, books, photographs and records relating the county's history. There is a complete pioneer kitchen, bedroom and living room. The museum is open Fridays and Saturdays from 12 to 4 pm. Located in downtown St. Helens, overlooking the Columbia River, the courthouse offers a fantastic view of the river and distant Mount St. Helens.

Two Industrial Towns from the mid-1800s

55 ♦ Just east of milepost marker 76, on US Highway 30, is a road leading north to two barely inhabited towns. To the east you'll encounter a weather-worn wooden bridge leading to the town of Bradwood. Once a busy company town, it was built in 1843 by the Bradley-Woodard Lumber Company. It is now just a sleepy collection of old homes.

If you turn west, you'll travel along the railroad tracks that run beside the river to Clifton. Remains here include a long-abandoned cannery and several old buildings. The first settlers arrived here in 1850, long before the railroad tracks were laid. Two pioneer salmon packers operated a cannery at this site.

Oregon Trail Mountain Route

In 1845, Samuel K. Barlow began a wagon route across the south shoulder of Mt. Hood. It was opened in 1846. This gave travelers an option to the dangerous journey down the Columbia River which cost so many pioneers their lives. It was the first dependable route over the Cascade Mountains. You can still find traces of the road today.

56♦ At Laurel Hill, just west of Government Camp, you can still see scars on the tree trunks where wagons were roped down slopes at several places. **Tollgate**, southeast of Rhododendron, is where the pioneers paid their fee for using Barlow's road. A replica of the original tollgate marks the spot, just east of Tollgate Campground.

57♦ The eastern gate was near Wamic. A narrow rough dirt road, portions can still be viewed. From Wamic, head south on Muller Road and turn right on Woodcock. Turn left on Smock Road and you will soon arrive at **Gate Creek**. This is where pioneer travelers found the first toll-gate. This starting point required a team of four oxen and enough supplies to last several months. By traveling along Forest Service Road 3530 you are following the actual route of Barlow Road. A nice side trip is found along Forest Service Road #013 leading to **Immigrant Springs**.

1896 Navigation Locks & Museum

58♦ The community of Cascade Locks is a **National Historic Site**. The town was an important stop for sternwheelers traveling up and down the Columbia River. You can still see the original 1896 navigation locks for which the city was named. They are located beside an aging canal. You can also walk along an **1872 wagon road** and visit a wonderful museum devoted to the history of the mighty sternwheeler. The museum is housed in the old lock-tender's residence.

At the **Cascade Locks Historical Museum** you will learn all about the important role the sternwheeler played in taming the Pacific Northwest. They also have the Pacific Coast's first steam locomotive, the Oregon Pony which began service here in 1862, as well as plenty of pioneer artifacts. The museum is open daily, June thru September, 12 to 5 pm Monday thru Wednesday and 10 am to 5 pm Thursday thru Sunday. They are open from 10 am to 5 pm weekends only, during the month of May.

Riverboat and Pacific Northwest Memorabilia

59♦ The Hood River Valley is known throughout the nation for its luscious apples and pears. At the **Hood River County Historical Museum** you can learn about the town's pioneer orchards and early fruit industry. Pioneer furnishings, Indian artifacts, military equipment, logging exhibits and county history are covered too. A number of special exhibits are also brought in each year. Outside you'll find weatherworn reminders of a time when people traveled mostly by river. The museum is open from mid-April thru October, Wednesday thru Saturday, from 10 am to 4 pm. On Sundays they close at 5 pm. To get there take exit #64 off I-84 at Hood River to Port Marina Park.

Hood River County Historical Museum

The End of the Original Oregon Trail

60 ♦ Between 1843 and 1846 The Dalles marked the end of the overland route for pioneers making their way west along the Oregon Trail. It was at this point that they converted their covered wagons into schooners for the dangerous journey down the raging river. The establishment of a toll road over the mountains in 1847 saved many lives and extended the overland trail westward. The later building of dams along the Columbia River has slowed the river to a less frantic pace.

In 1854, The Dalles became the county seat of the largest county ever formed in the United States. Wasco County was created in 1854 and originally included 130,000 square miles. The **original Wasco County Courthouse**, now located at 406 West Second, was built in 1859. It housed the sheriff's office and three jail cells on the lower floor; an outside stairway led to the second floor courtroom. Visitors today will find displays on local history, antique furniture and restored jail cells complete with thick wooden doors. Old wagons sit out front. This historic building is open from 11 am to 3 pm during April, May, September and October; summer hours are 10 am to 5 pm.

Many historic buildings constructed prior to the turn of the century still exist in The Dalles. The **1897 St. Peter's Catholic Mission** can be found at Third and Lincoln. Constructed of red brick, it is pure Gothic in style and includes graceful stone steps. The steeple, towers 176' above the ground and is now topped by a 6' weathervane rooster. The inside of the building is a monument of marble and stained glass. The church has been deconsecrated and can be toured weekdays from 11 am to 3 pm, weekends from 1 to 3 pm.

Original Wasco County Courthouse

A drive around town will reveal many other historic homes and buildings. Most are Victorian or Italianate in style. A few date from the 1860s. The clock tower on Third belongs to the second former county courthouse, built in 1883.

Other historical buildings in The Dalles include the following: on East Second Street you'll find an 1890 Hotel (200), 1879 Bank (300), 1870 Dry Goods Store (306), 1890 Casino (310), 1883 Bookstore (315), 1910

Department Store (321), and 1904 Lodge Buildings (421). Lovely historic homes exist on West Second Place - 420 (1878), 422 (1893), 406 (1879); West Third Place - 415 (1878), 505 (1895); West Fourth Street - 402 (1880), 316 (1868), 218 (1867); and West Sixth Street - 608 (1899). The homes can only be viewed from the street.

Oregon Trail Ruts

61 ♦ You can still see parts of the actual Oregon Trail in a couple of places in eastern Oregon. Imagine the wagon traffic it took to carve ruts so deeply into the earth that they are still there 150 years later. Southeast of Biggs, beside the road that parallels I-84, is one such spot. Near milepost marker 7 you will find a historic marker; about one mile further a dark wooden post marks the **Oregon Trail**. If you walk in, just a bit, you can see the remains of part of the 2,000 mile trail used by pioneer wagons.

Deschutes State Park, 6 miles west of Biggs, has an excellent **Oregon Trail Exhibit** relating the rich history of this area. The trail crossed the hazardous Deschutes River at this point. The wagons, also known as prairie schooners, were floated across while the livestock swam.

Just past the bridge, turn left to **Heritage Landing Park** along Old Moody Road. This gravel road will take you under a railroad bridge, past beautiful old barns and along a high bluff overlooking Celilo to Fairbanks. This is where the Oregon Trail started to parallel Fifteen Mile Creek. Look carefully to the right for another Oregon Trail marker.

62 ♦ Shaniko is Oregon's best ghost town! It was once a major city and the terminus of the Columbia Southern Railroad. Populated prior to the 1880s, the townsfolk here once supplied area sheepherders and railroad men with a variety of wares. Freight wagons and stage coaches bringing wool, sheep, cattle, gold and homesteaders came to Shaniko in great numbers. At its heyday this town boasted 13 saloons.

Turn-of-the-century Shaniko Hotel

Still standing, is the two-story brick Shaniko Hotel, the 1902 three-room schoolhouse and a good portion of the town proper. The early firehouse, an old livery barn, the marshal's office and a large wagon yard all remain. Shaniko is located just off State Highway 97, about 10 miles south of the Oregon/Washington border.

Old Shaniko School

Downtown Shaniko

Old Cars & Sheep Ranching History

63 ♦ Old cars ranging from an early Model T to a 1940 Packard are among the beauties on exhibit at the **Asher Old Car Museum** in Fossil. This wonderful little museum will delight car buffs! Fossil, with a population of about 500, is not the kind of town that pops up on most travel itineraries, but this car museum is a good reason why it should! Asher's is located on First Street, between Main and Washington, in the town's old blacksmith shop. It is open daily from April to October 8 am to 6 pm. At other times during the year it is open by request; ask at the city museum across the street.

Old cars - Fossil

The **Fossil City Museum** is filled with memorabilia relating the early history of an area settled prior to the 1870s. Sheep ranching was the chief industry here at that time and this museum is a great place to learn about its role in settling the area. You will also find displays on local settlers and pioneers. It is open daily, 8 am to 6 pm.

19th Century Clocks, Lamps & Bottles

64 ◆ The **Heppner Museum** is packed with historic memorabilia. Display cases filled with antique bottles, lamps, china and glass are found in the first room. Clocks from the early 19th century, antique medical instruments, frightful looking dental tools and old drug bottles are there as well.

Other items on display include old military uniforms, Indian artifacts, rocks and minerals, antique furnishings and quilts plus a section of the old Ione Post Office. The large South Room contains five recreated late 19th and early 20th century rooms, a bedroom, kitchen, parlor, dining room and music room. The museum's picture room is filled with oil paintings, pencil sketches, water colors and photographs. There is also a natural history room.

Outside, you'll find a one-room school house along with its little outhouse. These were in use from 1880 to 1940 at Democrat Gulch. A millstone from the area's first flour mill, built in 1874, is set into the lawn near the school house. The museum is located in Heppner, on North Main Street, next to the city park. Hours are 1 to 5 pm Monday, Wednesday, Thursday, Saturday and Sunday.

1870s Stagecoach Town

65 ♦ Twenty miles south of Heppner is one of Eastern Oregon's numerous living ghost towns; once flourishing cities with an ever-diminishing population. **Hardman** was settled in the 1870s and was an important stagecoach stop during its heyday. The town was originally named Dairyville but more commonly known as Raw Dog or Yellow Dog. When the community opened its post office in 1881 it was renamed Hardman, after a pioneer ranching family. The town flourished until the 1920s. Today only a few structures and people remain. Hardman is located along State Highway 207.

Five Eastern Oregon Ghost Towns

66 ♦ The area around Condon has lots of living ghost towns. **Lonerock**, 22 miles southeast of Condon, is a fine example. Named for the one huge rock that dominates an otherwise flat valley, the area was settled prior to the 1880s. A tiny Baptist church built before the turn of the century and the 1898 Methodist church are both still standing. A deserted main street, jail and area homes stand in various stages of decay. To reach Lonerock, leave State Highway 206 about 5 miles east of Condon and head southeast 16 miles.

67 ♦ **Olex** is another one of Eastern Oregon's nearly deserted ghost towns. Established in 1874, it contains an old country school, Jeremiah Crum's Mill, a cemetery and some old buildings. Olex is north of Condon about 20 miles, just west of State Highway 19.

68 ♦ Settled in 1890, today, **Richmond** is a barely inhabited collection of aging buildings. You'll find them just off State Highway 207, four miles southwest of its junction with State Highway 19. Still standing are a house with a corner porch, the still-handsome Methodist Church and a long building that once housed the post office, a boarding house and general store. The long building has a covered porch running along the entire front and may well have been Oregon's first mall. On the hillside, northwest of town, stand several large homes. Most are vacant, except for the small critters that can be heard scurrying about.

All three of these towns have residents whose very existence keeps these once thriving towns alive. Visitors should respect their privacy and property.

69 ♦ The town of **Antone** was named for a Portuguese pioneer settler. To find it take US Highway 26 west of Dayville four miles and head southwest on the gravel road leading toward Pine Hollow and Rock Creek. The buildings of this 1860s settlement straddle a creek. The little structure between the two frame houses served as a post office from 1894 to 1948.

If you want to explore another old site, keep following this road south. Stay left whenever the road Ys or meets another road and after a few hours you'll end up back at Highway 26. Along the way you'll pass by the **Spanish Gulch** cemetery, a square fort-like structure down a steep canyon. The square house was once a home and the canyon the center of local gold mining mania. Many abandoned homesteads, including one known as "Murderer's Cabin", dot the gorges of upper Rock Creek.

Courthouse Museum

70 ◆ In Madras you'll want to stop at the 1917 courthouse where you will find exhibits relating the history of local Indian tribes and pioneers. The **Jefferson County Museum** is open Thursday thru Saturday from 12 to 5 pm. Behind the courthouse you'll find the county's first jail. The small box-like structure with its barred windows and metal shutters is now used only for storage. The museum is located at 503 D Street.

Turn-of-the-Century Bank & Museum

71 ◆ Prineville was founded in 1868 with the erection of a blacksmith shop and saloon. These makeshift buildings were made up of pieces of abandoned covered wagons. Although the original buildings are gone, the city still has enough historic buildings to qualify for entry in the Historical Register of Properties. At the **Crook County Historical Society Bowman Museum**, 246 North Main, you can learn all about the town's strange beginnings.

The museum is in an old stone building that originally housed the town's bank. Inside you will find the original vault, wrought iron teller windows and sturdy marble counters. Indian arrowheads, pioneer furniture, antiques and hundreds of historic treasures are on exhibit here. The museum is open from March thru December, 10 am to 5 pm during the week and Saturdays 12 to 5 pm.

Authentic 1863 Guardhouse

72 ♦ **Fort Klamath** was established in 1863. This frontier military post was an important place during the Modoc Indian War of 1872-73. The fort's original guardhouse has been saved and now houses the **Fort Klamath Museum**. It contains Indian and pioneer memorabilia. You can visit the museum throughout the summer, 10 am to 6 pm daily.

Largest U.S. Display of Old Logging Equipment

73 ♦ The United States' largest logging equipment museum is found 33 miles north of Klamath Falls. Open year round, the **Collier Logging Museum** includes a wondrous collection of old logging equipment, steam locomotives and tractors, horse-drawn logging sleighs, a steam donkey engine and numerous log cabins. In all, you'll find more than 500 exhibits.

This impressive collection is located in **Collier State Park** which covers 350 acres at the junction of the Williamson River and Spring Creek. The park is located north of Chiloquin along US Highway 97.

As long as you're in the area, why not stop at the Chiloquin City Hall for a chance to learn about the region's original settlers. There you'll find the **Klamath Indian Memorial Museum** and learn the history of this great tribe. Throughout the summer the exhibits are open daily between 1 and 5 pm. Winter hours are 1:30 to 5 pm Tuesdays and Thursdays only.

Hot Spring History & Early Klamath Falls

74 ◆ You'll learn more about the Klamath Indians at the **Klamath County Museum** in Klamath Falls. Wildlife, logging, military conflicts and early pioneers are also covered. I was fascinated to learn how the Indians and early settlers used the abundant local hot springs for preserving and preparing foods, heating, bathing and medicinal purposes. The museum itself is supplied with free heat from a well drilled into the vast geothermal pocket located directly below its building.

You will also learn about George Nurse who in 1867 founded Klamath Falls, then known as Linkville. Other displays show the artistry of the Klamath and Modoc Indians who excelled in basket weaving, the importance of water transportation in the settlement of Klamath Falls and why ranchers came to the area. Historical photos include terrific shots of the city's 1907 horse drawn streetcar, calvary troops at Fort Klamath prior to the Modoc Indian War and turn-of-the-century harvest operations. The museum is located at 1451 Main Street and open Tuesday thru Saturday. Winter hours are 9 am to 5 pm, during the summer they stay open until 6 pm.

High Desert Ghost Towns

75 ◆ **Blitzen** is just one abandoned town among many in the high desert country. Deserted in 1917, it is a grim reminder of the many homesteaders who were unsuccessful in the dry Catlow Valley. You can find its remains southeast of Frenchglen. Take Blitzen Road 12.5 miles south, turn right and keep to the left for another 8.3 miles. The sagebrush trail will lead you to the deserted town.

76 ◆ **Narrows** is another deserted town. Once a lively village, it was started in 1892 by C. A. Haines. A few turn-of-the-century buildings still stand. You'll find them north of Frenchglen about 34 miles, near Harney and Malheur Lakes. If you take the Double O Road, one mile past the Narrows Bridge, and travel six miles you'll come across a small **pioneer cemetery**. It holds the grave of a child who died in 1845 while traveling with Meek's Lost Wagon Train. About one mile before you get to the cemetery you'll see a collection of **Indian pictographs**. The paintings are done in red pigment and include a six-legged lizard.

Indian Petroglyphs & 1880s Cattle Ranch

77 ◆ **Indian Artwork** was once found throughout the state. Much of it has been lost to thieves, vandals and the ravages of time. Petroglyphs are carvings made by Native Americans and were often tinted with dyes made from local plants. You can view a small collection of petroglyphs northeast of Frenchglen. Follow State Highway 205 north 18 miles toward

Central Point Road. Just south of the road you'll see a number of rimrocks and caves once used for shelter by local Indians. One has been partially excavated by archaeologists who found a smoke-blackened ceiling, grinding motors and obsidian flakes. The petroglyphs are etched on a large boulder near Krumbo Reservoir.

To visit the historic ranch turn right on Central Patrol Road. The ranch is 11.5 miles; follow the signs marked Malheur Wildlife Refuge substation.

In 1872 an enterprising young man, Peter French, came to eastern Oregon to buy land in the valley near present day Frenchglen. His spread, **P Ranch**, later became one of the most famous properties in the West. Much of the original ranch still stands. The best-known feature is its huge, **1880s round barn**. Built prior to 1884, the structure includes 250 tons of lava stones that were hauled from the Diamond Craters area. The barn is 100' in diameter and requires nearly 50,000 shingles to cover the roof.

Besides the round barn, you can also see the old beef wheel, restored willow corrals, long barn, original chimney and a fire tower where vultures come to roost at sunset. The cattle baron's empire now serves as a substation for the Malheur Wildlife Refuge.

Eastern Oregon Pioneer History

78 ◆ The town of Burns was established about 1883 when two local merchants moved their business from the nearby town of Egan. At the **Harney County Historical Museum**, 18 West "D" Street, you can learn all about those two pioneer businessmen. You'll also see exhibits of pioneer artifacts and household furnishings brought over the Oregon Trail, equipment from the old Hines Lumber Company, an antique printing press, a primitive hospital operating table, heirloom quilts and Indian arrowheads. The museum is open from June thru October. Hours are 9 am to 5 pm Tuesday thru Friday and 9 am to 12 pm on Saturdays.

Pioneer Wagon Trail

79 ◆ A number of smaller side trails were used by pioneers to find their promised land after the long treacherous trip over the Oregon Trail. Parts of one such trail can still be seen north of Juntura, at Beulah Reservoir. Located at the northeast end of the reservoir, the old wagon trail is marked by deep grooves. These grooves were probably first used during the 1840s, yet they are still quite visible 150 years later.

A Collection of Gold Mining Ghost Towns

The **Sumpter Mining District** is located east of Baker City and north of State Highway 7. This area was once filled with gold-mining towns. Only a few remains can be easily spotted today; many more towns have totally disappeared.

80 ◆ Southwest of Sumpter, the town of **Austin** was established in the late 1800s. Today only a few of the old buildings still stand. They are located about two miles north of US Highway 26, just off State Highway 7. Nearby **Bonanza** is marked by some decayed buildings and defunct hardrock mines. To reach it, take County Road #1030 off State Highway 7.

Galena and **Susanville** are located west of Austin. Follow State Highway 7 one mile north of its junction with US Highway 26 and turn left on the road that parallels the river. The two townsites are about 16 miles from here. After about 14 miles you'll meet up with another road. The right fork leads to Susanville. Go straight ahead and you'll reach Galena.

The first group of miners settled the Galena/Susanville area in 1862 when gold nuggets weighing as much as five pounds were found. Thousands of people lived in the area. Several old residences and a couple of stores still stand on the south side of the road. Up the narrow Elk Canyon are more remains. The old stamp mill and other buildings are spread out over nearly a mile.

81 ♦ Not much remains of **Whitney**, but a few of its original buildings still represent the days when it was a primary station on the narrow gauge Sumpter Valley Railroad. The town was almost totally deserted in 1918 when the sawmill located here burned. Remains of the mill can be seen at the log pond.

82 ♦ At **Greenhorn**, west of Sumpter and north of State Highway 7, you can see the remains of the old jail and a few early cabins. Another small town, Robinsonville, stood nearby. It was a typical gold rush town with 26 saloons. Fire swept thru the town at the end of the 19th century leaving little behind. Many mines dotted the area. At the Lazy Man Mine, the miner built his cabin directly over his mine shaft.

83 ♦ Granite was founded in the late 1860s and was originally known as Independence. Reminders of the old days include a schoolhouse, market, drug store, nickelodeon and cemetery. The town is located off Route 220, about 15 miles west of Sumpter. The population here was once nearly 5,000. Deteriorated buildings line main street. The largest served as a combination saloon, boardinghouse and community hall with a dance floor occupying the entire upper level.

North of Granite you can see rock walls in the stream bottom. These were made over 100 years ago by Chinese miners as they moved the large boulders to work up the finer gravel and sand underneath.

84 ♦ Sumpter was settled during the Civil War and at one time had three newspapers, a school system, an opera house, numerous stores and 15 saloons and brothels. The town's population was more than 3,000 in 1896. A fire destroyed most of the buildings in 1917. The Sumpter Valley Historical Railroad Park has the train that once transported the region's gold and timber to market. It now runs through the Sumpter Valley dredge tailings, which is protected as a wild game reserve. There is a charge to ride the train.

85 ♦ Bourne lies seven miles north of Sumpter, off State Highway 7. It was originally named Cracker City in the 1870s. A flash flood in 1937 wiped out most of the older buildings, but a few on higher ground remain along with some of the old equipment and mines. At one time, Cracker City was one of the major gold-producing centers at one time. The burned hulk of a gold mining dredge lies .5 mile north of the junction of State Highway 7 and Cracker Creek Road. Bourne is also the site of what was once thought to be the longest continuous gold vein in the world.

Eastern Oregon's Best Free Museum

86 ◆ The **Eastern Oregon Museum** in Haines is eastern Oregon's best museum and quite possibly my favorite. Its collection absolutely fills the old high school gym. They have a turn-of-the-century parlor and kitchen which also serves as a place to get warm during cooler months, plus endless aisles of implements and relics from the old west. One section, where children can play, holds nothing but long-forgotten toys. They also have the entire Bourne Bar from one of the area's gold-rush towns.

Outside is an 1880s Union Pacific depot and lots of antique equipment, both horse and steam-powered. The museum is easy to find and open daily, mid-April thru October, from 9 am to 5 pm.

Jackplanes, Chinese Artifacts & Antique Quilts

87 ◆ The town of Union was founded in 1862 and named in support of the Civil War's Union Army. When Union County was formed two years later it took its name from this town. Union has some delightful old Victorian homes and buildings. Privately owned, they are not open to the public but beautiful to view from the street. The town is small, you'll have no trouble finding them. The cemetery at the end of East Fulton Street was established in 1875 and has a number of classic Victorian head stones. The earliest marker is dated 1863; the oldest section is located in the northeast corner.

You'll learn all about the town's patriotic beginnings at the **Union County Museum**. Housed in a 19th century bank building, it also features Indian artifacts, pioneer belongings, jackplanes, hundred-year-old quilts, farm equipment and Chinese artifacts. The museum is located on Main Street and open from May thru October. Hours are 1 to 5 pm Thursday thru Monday.

Pondosa Ruins

88 ♦ Just off State Highway 203, 20 miles southeast of Union, is Pondosa, a deserted lumber town. Named for the lumber produced in the area, it became a ghost town when the industry could no longer support the mill. Although this area was settled earlier, the post office was not established until 1927. The ruins of the Grand Ronde Pine Company mill along with a few other buildings, make Pondosa an interesting stop.

Halfway Area Ghost Towns

89 ♦ The mines in the Halfway area were once considered to be in Oregon's most productive gold lode. Deteriorating buildings and old mining equipment can still be seen throughout the area. The town of **Cornucopia** was first occupied around 1885. You'll find its remains 11 miles northwest of Halfway on Cornucopia Road.

90 ♦ The town of **Homestead** is reached by driving 17 miles northeast of Halfway along State Highway 86. At Copperfield, go an additional four miles north. The town was established about 1900 by the owner of the Iron Dyke Mine. All that remains are some old copper mines and several aging buildings.

91 ♦ At **Sparta**, another former mining town, structures still standing include the old post office and a stone store building. There were settlers in this area as early as 1863; and Sparta is still inhabited by a few hardy souls. You'll find this living ghost town almost due west of Halfway. Follow State Highway 86 southwest 11 miles then head northwest on the Sparta Road 16 miles to the townsite.

The gravel road that runs from Sparta to Medical Springs will take you past **Sanger**. There you'll find an old hotel plus several other original buildings. Early records show the town was founded about the same time as Sparta. The Sanger mine was one of the largest gold producers in the area.

92 ♦ You can learn more about this historic gold mining area at the **Pine-Valley Community Museum** in Halfway. Reconstructed mining equipment, pioneer memorabilia and antique farming equipment are all included in the displays. The museum is open weekends only throughout the summer from 10 am to 4 pm.

The Ancestral Home of the Nez Perce Indians

93 ♦ The lands surrounding Joseph were the ancestral home of a famous band of Nez Perce Indians led by Chief Joseph. The Nez Perce had wintered in the Hell's Canyon area for 120 centuries. Carvings, rock faces and paintings have been found throughout. They lived here, in relative luxury, on the abundant game and plentiful fish. When settlers came to take over their homelands the tribe went to war. The battle, and their refusal to be ripped from their land and locked up on reservations, took them up into Canada. Each July the town of Joseph hosts a week long celebration known as **Chief Joseph Days**. Many of the events are free.

Non-Indian settlers began arriving in the Wallowa Lake area prior to the 1880s. Some of their original buildings still stand. The town's most prominent building was constructed in 1888 and now houses the **Wallowa County Museum**. Inside you'll find a number of exhibits relating the history of the Nez Perce. Pioneer settlers are also covered. The museum is open from Memorial Day until the third week in September from 10 am to 5 pm.

1880s Ghost Town

94 ♦ North of Enterprise about 35 miles is yet another of the region's living ghost towns. The old hotel, school house, general store and other aging buildings stand just as they did prior to the turn of the century. Named after the postmaster's daughter, **Flora** is still inhabited by a few hardy souls. You'll find it just west of State Highway 3, 10 miles south of the Washington/Oregon border.

Turn-of-the-Century Weston

95 ♦ Weston is the second oldest town in Umatilla County. The first post office was established here in 1867. Buildings built between 1879 and 1910 of locally made bricks dot the streets. You feel like you've stepped back in time. This community once supported four livery stables and two hotels.

Tour the town. Visit the library, town hall and museum buildings. At the library you'll see old photographs and maps of the area. The town hall was once a bank and still contains the original vault and etched teller windows. The museum has old paintings, an antique buggy and fire fighting equipment. You'll have to stop at City Hall to arrange for a tour of the museum. Weston is not a tourist attraction yet; its streets are still uncluttered. Stop by and get acquainted with the past.

1909 Railroad Depot & Museum

96 ♦ Pendleton's **Union Pacific Railroad Depot** is listed on the National Register of Historic Places. Built in 1909, it's made of red brick with flaring eaves and a tiled roof. No longer in use as a train depot, the interior has been renovated and now serves as a museum. The **Umatilla County Historical Society Museum** features a wonderful collection of artifacts. It's a great place to learn the history of the county which was founded in 1862. Pendleton is the county seat and got its start as a trading center around 1851. The museum is located at 108 SW Frazer and open Tuesday thru Saturday from 10 am to 4 pm.

Umatilla County Historical Society Museum

Oregon Trail Wagon Ruts

97 ♦ The Oregon Trail is still visible in several places across the state. South of Hermiston you can see where the trail crossed Butter Creek before making its way west to the town of Cecil. The wagon ruts are easy to see. You'll find them 14 miles south of

Hermiston, alongside State Highway 207. The **Oregon Trail Interpretive Center** in Cecil is also packed with historic information. Cecil is located along State Highway 74, southwest of Hermiston.

WASHINGTON'S BEST FREE
HISTORIC ATTRACTIONS

WASHINGTON MAP

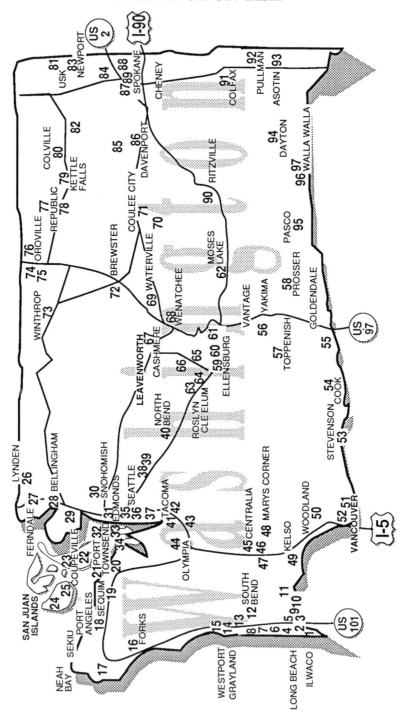

WASHINGTON

West Coast's Oldest Lighthouse

1 ♦ The oldest lighthouse on the West Coast is still operating atop a rocky headland at the mouth of the Columbia River. The beam from the **1856 Cape Disappointment Lighthouse** can be seen for 20 miles. These treacherous waters are littered with sunken ships; schooners, steamers, supply ships, gunboats, whalers and trollers are among those lost here.

Cape Disappointment was selected as a priority lighthouse site in 1848, but the construction experienced numerous setbacks. The biggest came in 1853 when the ship carrying building materials sank two miles off shore. It took another three years to get new materials and finish construction. A second lighthouse was added in 1898 due to a growing number of shipwrecks along the peninsula. The **North Head Lighthouse** is two miles north of the Cape Disappointment light.

To reach the lighthouses, leave Ilwaco heading west. After about 2 miles you'll find the North Head Lighthouse Trail. It's an easy walk. The Cape Disappointment Lighthouse Trail is another mile down the road. There are two ways to reach this light. Both are steep, but the old Coast Guard road is a shorter walk.

Old Fort Canby's Lewis and Clark Museum

2 ♦ Fort Canby protected the southern Washington coast from the mid-1800s until 1957. It now serves as a state park. Although the fort's original buildings are gone, a few of the concrete bunkers and batteries can still be seen.

The modern two-story building overlooking Cape Disappointment is where you'll find the **Lewis and Clark Interpretive Center**. Its wonderful exhibits take you from the journey's early planning stages to the expedition's first view of the Pacific Ocean in 1805. The building of Fort Canby, construction of the cape's historic lighthouses and details about the area's many shipwrecks are also covered.

The center is open from May thru mid-September; call (206) 642-3078 for current hours. **Fort Canby State Park** is located a couple of miles west of Ilwaco; simply follow the signs. The park is open from April thru mid-October, during daylight hours.

Miniature Turn-Of-The-Century IRN Railroad

3 ♦ Railroad buffs will particularly enjoy the **Ilwaco Heritage Foundation Museum** train depot gallery. This restored depot houses a miniature railroad display that is an exact replica of the Long Beach Peninsula in 1920. It includes 2,500 tiny trees, exact replicas of the area's historic homes, businesses and other landmarks plus a working model of the old IRN train.

Other displays and galleries cover early telephones, radio communication and regional history. You'll also find lots of information about the area's Native American inhabitants and early settlers. The Discover and Exploration Gallery contains maps and navigational instruments used to chart the Northwest coast as well as fur trade artifacts and pioneer goods.

The museum is located in Ilwaco at the convention center, on Lake Street. It is open year round, 9 am to 4 pm Monday thru Saturday, plus summer Sundays from 12 to 4 pm.

Jake the Alligator Man and Other Oddities

4 ♦ For my family, a trip to the Long Beach Peninsula without a stop at **Marsh's Free Museum** is just not possible! It's a fun place for kids of all ages and literally filled with unusual, unbelievable, odd and just plain fun items as well as a variety of historic artifacts. If the weather turns gloomy, this is a great place to while away the hours.

Marsh's has a number of fascinating antique coin-operated music boxes and the world's most unique collection of glass balls, as well as shrunken heads, and the remains of Jake the Alligator Man. You'll also find shipwreck artifacts, authentic Indian canoes, old farm tools and a stuffed two-headed pig. You won't want to miss it!

This wonderful museum is located right in Long Beach; it's impossible to miss. It's open year round from 9 am to 6 pm, during the summer months they often stay open until 9 or 10 pm.

Historic Long Beach Peninsula

The Long Beach Peninsula has been a seaside resort area since the 1800s. Many of its towns began as fishing villages and oyster harvesting operations. Today you can still see a number of original buildings along the peninsula. Most are privately owned and can only be viewed from the road.

5 ◆ **Ilwaco** and **Seaview** include a number of Victorian homes from the 1880s. The towns' back streets are where you'll find the real treasures.

6 ◆ At **Klipsan Beach** the 1889 Lifesaving Station provided aid to the area's mariners for nearly 60 years. This collection of nine historic buildings is now privately owned. The town also features some wonderful turn-of-the-century beach cottages. To the north, at **Ocean Park**, historic buildings include the old Taylor Hotel and 1889 Matthews-Whalebone House on Bay Avenue, as well as the unusual Wreckage built in 1912 from local flotsam and jetsam.

7 ◆ **Nahcotta** was once the terminus for a narrow gauge railway completed in 1889. The train depot and original post office still stand. Even though the train hasn't run for over a half century, the train schedule is still posted on the side of the post office building.

8 ◆ The **Oysterville Historic District** protects a number of lovely old buildings near the peninsula's northern end. Once the center of the local oyster industry, Oysterville was also the original county seat. The **Oysterville Cemetery** is filled with Pacific County pioneers. During the boom days, 1855 to 1893, this lively town had two hotels, five saloons, a weekly newspaper and a college. You can get a walking tour map at the Oysterville Church.

9 ♦ Just west of the Astoria Bridge, on Highway 101, you'll see the beautiful **1904 St. Mary's Catholic Church**. The **Lewis & Clark campsite** is just a stone's throw from here. A marker points the way to the spot where the expedition camped in November of 1805. Nearby **Chinook** contains several splendid 19th century homes built when it was the richest town per capita in the United States.

1897 Army Fort

10 ♦ **Fort Columbia** is a beautifully preserved turn-of-the-century army base. Original structures include defense batteries, bunkers, lookouts, search light stations, hospital, barracks, officers' quarters, fire station, guardhouse, supply building and theater. The

Concrete defense batteries - Fort Columbia

fort was an important base during the Spanish American War as well as World Wars I and II. It now serves as a public recreation area. Kids especially enjoy exploring the underground bunkers.

Barracks - Fort Columbia

Inside the 1902 Enlisted Men's Barracks you can see how the soldiers lived. You'll also find exhibits on the development of this region and the importance of the fort. This is a great place to start your tour. The former Commandant's Quarters has been furnished much as it was at the turn of the century and the old Quartermaster's Storehouse houses the **Chinook Observer Printing Museum**.

You'll find the fort west of the Astoria toll bridge, near Chinook. Park hours are 6:30 am to dusk April thru mid-October; the balance of the year they open at 8 am. During the winter the fort is closed on Mondays and Tuesdays. Call (206) 642-3078 for current museum hours.

Washington's Last Useable Covered Bridge

11 ◆ Washington's covered bridges have almost entirely disappeared. In fact, there is only one covered bridge in the state that is still in use. You'll find it east of the Long Beach Peninsula, at Grays River. Built in 1905, the **Grays River Covered Bridge** crosses the gently flowing Grays River surrounded by farmlands.

Grays River Covered Bridge

The Town That Stole The County Seat

12 ◆ According to the residents of Oysterville, South Bend stole the county seat in 1893. South Bend residents claim they legally won it in the 1892 election but were forced to send two steamers to "kidnap" the county records. This colorful history just adds to the charm of a visit to the **1911 South Bend County Courthouse**.

South Bend County Courthouse

This is one of the most beautiful courthouses in the state with its sensational art glass dome, extensive ornamental features and fascinating wall paintings. You can tour the building during business hours.

The Chinook Indians called Willipa Bay home for many centuries. At the **Pacific County Historical Museum** on US Highway 101 you can learn all about this skillful tribe. Pioneer and regional history is also well covered. During the summer they are open daily between 11:30 am and 4:30 pm; the balance of the year Monday, Wednesday, Friday and Saturday only from 11:30 am to 3:30 pm .

In Remembrance Of The Early Cranberry Picker

13 ♦ The misty sea climate, ancient peat bogs and surface ground water around Grayland makes it one of the major cranberry suppliers in the US. The local cranberry bogs were started around 1915 and are still thriving. At the **Furford Cranberry Museum** you can see the early tools and equipment used when this West Coast operation was young.

This is really a fun and friendly place to stop. The museum was established by Julius Furford, a local man who invented the gas-powered harvesting machine. His invention ended the back breaking job of crawling thru the wet bogs with wooden-toothed scoops combing the vines for ripe berries.

The museum is housed in an old dance pavilion and has lots of other antiques as well. Treadle sewing machines, gas powered washing machines, Edison gramophones, victrolas, logging and shipbuilding tools are all found here. Located near the north end of Grayland, off State Highway 105, it's a great place to spend an hour or two. The museum is open weekends only, throughout the summer, between 10 am and 4 pm.

Maritime, Military and Indian History

14 ♦ The **Westport Maritime Museum** is housed in an old Coast Guard station, in the center of the Westport dock area. The Nantucket-style building has roof-top cupolas and a widow's walk.

Westport Maritime Museum

Gray whale skeleton - Westport Maritime Museum

Inside you'll find military exhibits, maritime equipment, Indian artifacts, rock displays and lots of historic photographs. Outside you can view a fully assembled skeleton of a young gray whale and some aging Coast Guard equipment. This museum provides an excellent diversion if the weather turns rainy. History buffs will enjoy it any time.

Throughout the summer the museum is open Wednesday thru Sunday 12 to 4 pm. In April and May they are also open on weekends. The balance of the year you can only tour by appointment. Call (206) 268-9692.

Tour an 1898 Lighthouse

15 ♦ The **Grays Harbor Lighthouse**, built in 1898, is the tallest lighthouse on the Washington Coast. Its 107' tower houses a red/white light that can be seen 30 miles out to sea. Beneath the iron dome you'll find four tons of light assembly which can only be reached by climbing a 135-step circular staircase. Lighthouse tours must be arranged in advance; call (206) 268-0121 and ask for the Executive Petty Officer. To reach the lighthouse from Westport, take the road marked **Westport Light State Park**; off State Highway 105.

Ancient Trees and Pioneer Logging Exhibits

16 ♦ South of Forks you can visit an ancient rain forest. The **Hoh Rain Forest** receives over 145 inches of rain each year. Spruce trees in this old growth forest reach a height of over 300'.

At the **Forks Timber Museum**, just north of town, you can learn all about pioneer logging on the Olympic Peninsula. The museum is devoted to the old-time logging industry and includes lots of the original equipment. You'll also find pioneer goods, Indian artifacts and an authentic fire lookout tower. A short trail beside the museum provides an easy walk thru an old growth area.

The museum is open Tuesday thru Saturday 10 am to 6 pm and Sundays 1 to 5 pm from mid-April thru October. During November and December it is open weekends only; Saturdays from 10 am to 6 pm and Sunday from 1 to 5 pm.

2,000 Year Old Indian Village Site

17 ◆ Parts of the **Ozette Indian Village** were flattened and buried by mud flows over 500 years ago. This unique wet site has yielded entire houses preserved by the blue-gray clay. Other parts of the Ozette site, those not affected by mud flows, are believed to have been occupied up to 2,000 years ago. In all, over 50,000 items have been recovered from Ozette. Many of these artifacts are now displayed at the Makah Museum in Neah Bay. There is a charge to tour the museum but it's well worth the cost!

To reach the village site you have to hike 4 miles. From Sekiu, leave State Highway 112 heading southwest 36 miles to Lake Ozette. At the road's end, take the forest trail 3.5 miles west then head north up the beach for an additional .5 mile. This area offers outstanding views and a number of undisturbed tide pools as well.

Authentic Indian Long House and Local History

18 ♦ The Port Angeles area is rich in Native American and pioneer history. You'll find an authentic Indian long house at Lincoln Park, which is on West Lauridsen and Bean Road. This is the traditional house built by many Northwest tribes. The park also has a few pioneer log cabins.

Indian long house - Lincoln Park

The best place to learn about the region's pioneers is the **Clallam County Museum**. Located in the elegant **1914 county courthouse** on Lincoln Street, it is open weekdays, year round from 10 am to 4 pm. During the summer they are also open on Saturdays.

You'll find more pioneer exhibits at the **Olympic National Park Visitor Center** on South Race Street. Their **Pioneer Memorial Museum** covers the history of Clallam County and the Olympic Peninsula as well as area wildlife, plants and geology. The center opens daily at 8 am and closes at 4 pm; during the summer they stay open until 7 pm. It's a great place to learn about this unspoiled region.

Sequim-Dungeness Historical Attractions

19 ♦ Settlers first came to the Sequim area in 1851, settling at the base of Cline Spit in a place they called New Dungeness. You'll learn all about those early beginnings at the **Sequim-Dungeness Museum**, 175 Cedar Street. The museum also includes exhibits on local birds and waterfowl, marine specimens, mastodon bones, Indian artifacts and a collection of ship and lighthouse models. It's open Tuesday thru Sunday from mid-May to November, and Wednesday, Friday and Sunday the balance of the year. Hours are 12 to 4 pm.

If you're interested in old buildings, ask at the museum for a copy of the valley's scenic and old barn tour sheets. The first will lead you past some lovely old buildings including the **1892 Dungeness School House** and the **1861 McAlmond House**. The second tour sheet covers 29 miles and meanders past 25 old and new barns.

Port Townsend, An 1860s Seaport Town

20 ♦ History buffs will love Port Townsend. Both the downtown waterfront district and the original residential area have been designated **National Historic Districts**. The town is full of wonderful old waterfront structures and beautiful Victorian mansions. The majority of the town's gracious mansions, built between 1860 and the turn of the century, have been restored. Many serve the tourist industry.

Port Townsend

Maps showing the locations and history of Port Townsend's older homes and buildings are available around town. They show where to find the 1865 St. Paul Episcopal Church, 1893 Customs House, 1889 Hastings Building, 1874 Fowler Building, dozens of Victorian homes and mansions plus other historic sites.

Most of the town's Victorian homes are not open to the public. The **1868 Rothschild House** is an exception. This lovely home was built by an early Port Townsend merchant and can be toured daily, from April 15th thru October 15th, between 10 am and 5 pm. The house is open 11 am to 4 pm weekends and holidays only during the balance of the year. You'll find it at Franklin and Taylor, on the hill right behind the town center. Donations are heartily encouraged and there has been talk of instituting a charge here.

Rothschild House kitchen

The **Jefferson County Historical Museum** holds a fascinating collection. It's housed in the 1891 City Hall Building and fills three floors. In the basement you can visit a primitive jail cell where Jack London is said to have spent the night in 1897 on his way to the Alaskan gold fields.

The top floor is filled with Victorian toys, furniture and dolls. The main level holds a number of interesting collections. Old bottles, buttons, seashells, stuffed birds, fire fighting equipment, Chinese and Indian artifacts, military uniforms, Victorian furnishings, and thousands of historic photographs and paintings fill its rooms. You'll learn all about Port Townsend's pioneers, the Clallam and Makah Indian tribes, the city's early Chinese colony, it's rich maritime history and old Fort Worden. The museum is open Monday thru Saturday 11 am to 4 pm, Sundays 1 to 4 pm and also heartily encourages donations.

Jefferson County Historical Museum display

1897 Fort Worden

21 ♦ Point Wilson got its first military fort in 1855 when Fort Wilson was built to guard against Indian uprisings. The original fort was abandoned in 1856 and in 1897 Fort Worden was built there to protect the Puget Sound from foreign invasion. It was closed down shortly after the Korean War. The land and buildings are now part of Port Townsend's **Fort Worden State Park**.

This 330 acre estate features a collection of restored Victorian officers' houses, barracks, parade grounds and artillery bunkers. Historic features include abandoned gun emplacements, the **Point Wilson Lighthouse**, **Alexander's Castle** and the **US Government Cemetery**. Visitors can tour the **Commander's House** and the **248th Artillery Museum**; call (206) 385-4730 for current hours.

1852 Thomas Coupe Land Claim

22 ♦ Thomas Coupe was a sea captain who fell in love with Penn Cove, staking his claim to include the spot that is now known as Coupeville. This historic village is my favorite San Juan Islands' town with its authentic false-front buildings and handsome Victorian homes. Two of the original blockhouses built to defend the settlers from island Indians still stand in Coupeville. **Alexander Blockhouse**, built in 1855, is located at the end of Front Street. **Davis Blockhouse** is found near the cemetery.

Coupeville has been placed on both the State and National Historic Registers. A simple brochure outlining a walking tour past 45 historic buildings is available around town. Most of these lovely Victorian homes are privately owned and can only be viewed from the street. A great place to start your tour is at the east end of Front Street. This street includes the 1854 Coupe House, 1886 Clapp House, 1871 Kinney Home, 1866 Granville Haller House, 1871 Still House, 1852 Fairhaven log cabin and a number of false-front buildings.

Coupeville waterfront

Whidbey Island Historic Reserve

23 ♦ The **Ebey's Landing National Historic Reserve** protects a rural community teeming with historical sights. It provides an unbroken record from the time when Puget Sound was first explored and settled to the present. Ebey's Landing commemorates the visit by Captain George Vancouver, the first Island settlement by Colonel Isaac Neff Ebey prior to 1850, early island pioneers and homesteaders.

The historic town of Coupeville, Fort Casey State Park, Ebey's Landing, Grasser's Hill and Lagoon, Crockett Lake and Uplands, Monroe's Landing and Smith Prairie are all included within the reserve boundaries.

At **Fort Casey State Park** you can explore the remains of a sea-guarding fort built in the late 1890s. Once the fourth largest military post in the state, the property became part of the state parklands in 1956. The rehabilitated **Admiralty Head Lighthouse** is also found here. Tours of the lighthouse are available; call (206) 678-4519.

Ebey's Landing protects one of America's last primitive prairies; limited access is permitted. A drive along Keystone Spit, to the northwest corner of Crockett Lake, will take you to the **Crockett Blockhouse**. This is one of the four original blockhouses built by island pioneers.

The English-American Pig War Camps

When the Oregon Treaty was signed establishing a US/Canada boundary, neither side was clear on the ownership of San Juan Island. This led to a number of heated disputes and nearly brought the US and Great Britain to war in the late 1850s when an American killed a British owned pig he found rooting in his garden. At that time the island was inhabited by approximately 14 Americans and 7 British citizens.

On July 27, 1859, a company of 461 American soldiers were landed on the island's south end. In response, the British sent 5 ships and 2,000 men with orders to drive the Americans off the island. To avoid a war, terms of joint occupancy was established barring each side from having more than 100 men on the island while the boundary dispute was being settled. The British camp was set up on the island's northern end. That joint occupancy lasted 12 years.

24 ◆ Today you'll find two national parks on San Juan Island. They provide a detailed look at the 1859-72 Pig War. On the island's north end, the 529 acre **English Camp National Historic Park** includes three of the original buildings. A lovely woodland hike leads uphill to the camp cemetery.

25 ◆ The 1200 acre **American Camp National Historic Park** includes hiking trails and a number of historic sites near the Island's southern end.

Friday Harbor, on the island's eastern side, is where you'll find the **San Juan Historical Museum**. This lovely turn-of-the-century farm homestead is filled with items brought to the island by early settlers. Outside you'll find a wooden jail built in 1892 and a 1917 Cadillac fire truck. The museum is open Wednesday thru Saturday throughout the summer from 1 to 4:30 pm. The balance of the year it is open Thursday and Friday only from 1 to 4 pm.

Horseless Carriage and Wagon Collection

26 ◆ The **Lynden Pioneer Museum** contains a wonderful collection of both horse-drawn and horseless carriages. Wagons, carts and a variety of buggies restored to their original condition are the cornerstone of this small town museum. Antique cars include a collection of Chevrolets from 1914 to 1931.

Wagon collection - Lynden Pioneer Museum

Old town display - Lynden Pioneer Museum

Old tractors, steam operated farm machinery, Indian artifacts, military souvenirs and a turn-of-the-century theme street are a few more reasons why this museum is one of the best in the state. You'll find it all in Lynden at Third and Front Streets. They are open April thru October from 10 am to 5 pm Monday thru Saturday. The balance of the year they are open Thursday thru Saturday from 12 to 4 pm.

Ferndale's **Pioneer Park** is filled with log cabins built by local pioneers. The cabins have been relocated here, forming a small pioneer village along the Nooksack River. Their solid cedar walls are 12-24

Pioneer Park log church

inches thick and were hewn from logs using alder wedges and axes. These rectangular slabs were then set one on top of another, using a dovetail style borrowed from the Russian forts built along the coast. Tours are available from May thru September, between 12 and 5 pm.

The **1885 Shields House** was originally built at Wiser Lake. The Shields family built this two-story home themselves using timber found on their own land. It was considered quite large for the time. The logs were split and their ends mortised and dovetailed so precisely, that they interlocked and needed no nails. This is the most elaborate of the pioneer cabins and is furnished much like it may have been around the turn of the century.

The park also includes an **1876 log church**, **1870 granary**, the **Parker House** which operated as a hotel during the 1870s, 1895 Foster Cabin, **1877 Grandview House**, and the **1890 Homeman House**. The latter is outfitted as a one-room school house.

Historic Bellingham

28 ◆ Four separate towns once existed along Bellingham Bay. Overlapping growth eventually forced them to consolidate into a single city, Bellingham. The best preserved of those original cities is **Old Fairhaven** which was conceived in the 1880s by a smuggler. The town's 1890s buildings are being restored to their original beauty. To find Fairhaven from I-5, take exit #250. The Marketplace, at 12th and Harris, is a good place to start your historic tour.

Some of the state's oldest buildings still stand near the mouth of Whatcom Creek in downtown Bellingham. You'll find **Washington's oldest brick building** on E Street near Astor. Built in 1858, this was Whatcom County's second courthouse. **St. Paul's Episcopal Church** at 2117 Walnut has a parish hall that was built in 1885.

The **Eldridge Avenue Historic District** sports a number of impressive homes built between 1880 and 1910. Much of this area is listed on the National Register of Historic Places. Beautiful **Elizabeth Park** is the county's oldest park and a classic example of turn-of-the-century landscape architecture. To reach the Eldridge district leave the downtown area on F Avenue.

Old Sehome, on the northern shoulder of Sehome Hill, has an expansive collection of large turn-of-the-century homes. The original town of Bellingham is located at the neighborhood's south end. Many buildings in this area have actually been part of four towns, without ever moving. North Garden, East Maple, Forest and Main all feature historic buildings.

To learn more about Bellingham's original cities be sure to visit the **Whatcom Museum of History and Art**. Regional history and Northwest contemporary art occupy three floors at 121 Prospect Street in one of the loveliest Victorian buildings in the state. The building was designed by Alfred Lee and in 1892 served as New Whatcom's city hall.

Inside you'll find a historic photographic collection that includes 30,000 regional prints and negatives.

Whatcom Museum of History and Art

Eskimo, Aleut and Northwest Coast Indian artifacts
and ceremonial masks, plus a permanent collection of
contemporary works by Northwest artists can also be
seen. Other permanent exhibits cover birds of the
Northwest, the logging industry and Victorian

lifestyles. The museum offers 17 changing exhibits each year which showcase both art and history. They are open Tuesday thru Sunday 12 to 5 pm.

La Conner; A Step Back In Time

29 ♦ La Conner is a lovely little town that got its start as a fishing village on the banks of the Swinomish River 130 years ago. This is the oldest town in Skagit County and one of the oldest in the state. Its beginnings date to the early 1860s.

There are more than 161 historic buildings and sites in the **La Conner Historic District**. Most of the downtown area is listed on both the National and State Historic Registers. **Totem Pole Park** was the site of a trading post in 1868. At the park you can examine a 24' shovel-nose canoe carved by the Swinomish Indians, and an authentic totem pole.

The Tillinghast Seed Company is the oldest operating store in the Northwest. Their original 1890 headquarters is that wonderful old building you see as you enter town. The **Tillinghast Seed Company Museum** is filled with items from the company's first 100 years. A gallery displaying 100 years of seed catalogue covers, the company's ancient printing press with all its lead type, antique furnishings, scales and bins are all on display.

Lifestyles of 19th Century Snohomish

30 ♦ Snohomish is another wonderful little historic town. Once the crossroads for military road and steamboat river travelers, the red brick downtown area has changed little over time. The town is filled with elegant wooden frame houses, many dating from the 1890s.

The **Snohomish Historic District**, between First and Fifth Avenues, has dozens of lovely buildings. These include turn-of-the-century mansions, an old Opera House, saloon building, clinkerbrick house and the Blackman House. Privately owned, most of these homes can only be viewed from the street. Seven historic Snohomish churches, built between 1874 and 1898, can be visited on Sunday mornings.

The **Blackman House Museum**, 118 Avenue B, was built in 1878 by a local lumberman as a place to display the shingles made at his mill. The house has been beautifully restored and furnished with period antiques. It is open to the public on weekends, between 12 and 4 pm.

Near the intersection of State Highway 9 and Marshland Road, in a small park, you'll find a 500 year old cedar tree. Measuring 48' around, this old growth tree has had a pathway carved through its base since about the turn-of-the-century. Known as **The Bicycle Tree**, the pathway was hand cut by a logger for a fee of $15.

Sailing Ships & Pioneer History

31 ◆ Indian artifacts, old time musical instruments, antique guns, pioneer furniture and furnishings, logging, carpenter and shipwright tools plus hundreds of historic photographs are on display at the **Edmonds Museum**. A particular favorite with maritime enthusiasts are the marine displays which include photographs of early day vessels, ship models and nautical instruments. The museum is located in a beautiful 1910 brick and stone Carnegie library building at 118 Fifth Avenue North, in downtown Edmonds.

1853 Port Gamble

32 ♦ The entire town of Port Gamble has been designated a **National Historic Site**. Established in 1853 by Captain William Talbot as a sawmill town, the community sports a number of handsome buildings with an unusual New England architectural style.

On Main Street you'll find the original 1853 Post Office, 1870 Masonic Temple, 1870 Episcopal Church and a number of beautifully restored 19th century homes. The Thompson House, built in 1859, is the oldest continuously occupied house in the state. Other community highlights include the restored General Store and the sawmill itself. You don't need a map to explore Port Gamble, it's easy to see everything by just wandering down the main streets.

Kitsap Peninsula History

33 ♦ You can learn all about early Kitsap Peninsula settlers at Silverdale's **Kitsap County Historical Museum**. Exhibits include early day clothing, toys, clocks, musical instruments and nautical artifacts. A large collection of historic photographs are also on display. The museum is located at 3343 NW Byron Street and is open Tuesday thru Sunday between 1 and 4 pm.

Shipyard Museum & Graveyard

34 ♦ Carved bowsprits, ship models, naval artifacts and instruments as well as historic photos and drawings are on display at the **Puget Sound Naval Shipyard Museum**. This fine museum provides a great opportunity to learn about Puget Sound's intriguing shipyard history. It's open daily, 9 am to 5 pm.

This area was first selected as the site of a Navy shipyard in 1891. It is now one of the most important installations of its kind in America. A large portion of the Navy's battleships, carriers, destroyers and submarines are based in Pacific waters, and many call this shipyard home. You can see some of the older ships, known as the **mothball fleet**, at the shipyard's west end.

Gold Fever, Old Masters and Dinosaurs

35 ♦ The **Klondike Gold Rush National Historic Park** heralds old Seattle, the place prospectors came to begin the journey to the Klondike gold fields. This is where they bought supplies and boarded their ships in 1897-98 for the difficult journey to Alaska. Start your visit at the **Klondike Gold Rush Museum**, 117 S. Main Street. There you will learn all about the treacherous trail from Seattle to the gold fields up north, how the miners lived and see the crude tools they used.

You can learn all about Coast Guard history in the Pacific Northwest and Alaska at the **Northwest Coast Guard Museum**. This collection includes 2,500 historic artifacts, 9,000 photos and more than 2,000 articles, clippings and books. You'll find the museum at 1519 Alaskan Way South. It is open Friday thru Wednesday between 1 and 5 pm.

At the **Frye Art Museum**, 704 Terry, you'll find a wonderful collection of paintings by the old masters. This lovely museum was established by Charles and Emma Frye who willed the city 230 paintings and the funding necessary to build and operate a public art museum. Other works have been added since then. The museum is open 10 am to 5 pm Monday thru Saturday and 12 to 5 pm on Sundays.

The **University of Washington Museum** places a special emphasis on Pacific Northwest natural history. You'll find anthropology, geology and zoology displays here along with the most complete dinosaur skeleton collection on permanent display in the Pacific Northwest. Established in 1885, this is the oldest university museum still in operation in the West. Hours are 11 am to 5:30 pm Tuesday thru Friday and 9 am to 4:30 pm on weekends.

The **University Observatory** was built in 1895. The telescope was manufactured in 1891. Both are still in use and offer free viewing. Call (206) 543-2888 for the current schedule. You'll find the University at 4014 University Way N.E..

Ye Olde Curiosity Shop has lots of interesting oddities including a 6' mummy found in the Gila Bend Desert and a memorable shrunken head collection. Established in 1899, this is a fourth generation family operation. Antique weapons, Indian carvings, Chinese artifacts and ivory sculptures are also on display in this world famous collection. You'll find it at 601 Alaskan Way.

Historic Seattle

36 ◆ Most of Seattle's downtown area was rebuilt after a raging fire leveled the booming town in 1889. A total of 66 blocks were destroyed. Most of the buildings in the **Pioneer Square Historic District** date from 1889 to 1900. Architect Elmer H. Fisher was the designing mind behind the Pioneer Building and at least 60 others in Seattle. His work is primarily done in Romanesque Revival style. The historic district covers 25 city blocks, south of downtown.

A good place to start a walking tour is **Pioneer Square Park**, First and Yesler Streets. This has been a popular meeting place for over 100 years. Its little triangle of grass and cobblestones was once the heart of early Seattle. If you stop at 117 S. Main Street you can get a map of the historic district.

You'll find an exhibit containing more than 500 vintage photographs, maps and items relating Seattle's waterfront history at Ivar's Acres of Clams on Pier 54. This **historic waterfront photograph exhibit** includes a number of sailing and ferryboat photographs from the mid-1800s. Seattle's early residents, gold rush fever, war time hoopla and waterfront construction have also been captured in this pictorial display.

100 Year Old Lighthouse

37 ◆ The **Alki Point Light Station** was built more than 100 years ago. On weekends and holidays, between 1 and 4 pm, you can tour this historic lighthouse and chat with Coast Guard personnel. The light station is located in Seattle at 3201 Alki Avenue SW.

Historic Railroad Depot

38 ◆ In Snoqualmie you will often find early steam and electric trains at the historic **Snoqualmie Depot**.

Snoqualmie Railroad Depot

This restored train depot is the base of operation for the Puget Sound Railway Historical Association's Snoqualmie Valley Railroad. Although it costs to ride the trains, kids of all ages like to watch as these historic beauties leave the depot. These excursions run most summer weekends between Snoqualmie and North Bend. Inside the depot you will also find lots of railroad memorabilia.

Old-Time Logging & Pioneer Memorabilia

39 ♦ In North Bend you can see antique logging equipment used by pioneer loggers to harvest the valley's timber. It's fun to see the crude saws and heavy tools used by those early loggers. Pioneer artifacts belonging to Snoqualmie Valley settlers are also on display at the **Snoqualmie Valley Historical Museum**. Exhibits relate the hardships and lifestyles of the area's first non-Indian settlers. The museum is open weekends only, March thru October, from 1 to 5 pm.

1868 Wagon Road

40 ♦ In 1868 the **Snoqualmie Pass Wagon Road** was the only wagon route over the Cascade Mountains to Puget Sound. It was used by freight wagons and settlers. You can still see a 1 mile stretch of this historic road. To get there, leave I-90 about 17 miles southeast of North Bend and follow County Road #58 northeast 2.5 miles. The old road is near the Denny Creek Campground. You can get a self-guided tour booklet at the Snoqualmie Pass National Forest office.

41 ◆ Old Fort Nisqually is now part of Tacoma's **Point Defiance Park**. Among the restored 1854 fort buildings you'll find a refurbished shop, officers' house and several storehouses. Visitors are welcome in the fort between 11 am and 7 pm during the summer, 9 am to 5 pm the balance of the year. The **Fort Nisqually Museum** is open 1 to 4 pm and tells the tale of this Hudson Bay trading post's early days. On summer weekends you can also visit the fort's granary and blacksmith shop between 1 and 5 pm.

Fort Nisqually

This 700 acre public park has a beautiful 5 mile loop drive that winds thru a 500 acre **old growth forest**. A number of hiking trails and bicycle paths can be taken off this road. The loop also leads to several great viewpoints overlooking Puget Sound. Point Defiance Park also offers a number of attractions that are not cost free. Another free park attraction is the **1865 Job Carr Cabin**. You'll find it beside the Big Tree Trail. To reach the park take the Pearl Street exit off State Highway 16 and follow the signs.

Renoirs & Chinese art

42 ♦ The permanent collection at the **Tacoma Art Museum** includes works by Renoir, Degas and Pissarro as well as a number of fine American painters. I especially enjoyed the Chinese imperial robes and jade items and my daughter was fascinated with the Children's Gallery. You'll find this lovely museum at 1123 Pacific Avenue in downtown Tacoma. Hours are 10 am to 4 pm Monday thru Saturday and 12 to 5 pm on Sundays.

Military Museum

43 ♦ The **Fort Lewis Military Museum** is packed with items relating the Northwest's colorful military history. Old photographs, war posters, Army uniforms, old guns, military equipment and an array of weapons from local and national confrontations are all on display.

Outstanding exhibits include those devoted to early Pacific Northwest soldiers, World War I troops and the Ninth Infantry Division. Soldiers from 1804 to current times are covered. Outside you'll find a lot of military vehicles that were used prior to World War I plus some late model experimental attack vehicles.

The museum is open Wednesday thru Sunday, 12 to 4 pm, year round. It is closed on major holidays. To reach the museum take exit #120 off I-5 and follow the signs.

Capitol Mansion

44 ♦ The 32 room Lord mansion, 211 W. 21st Avenue, is the site of Olympia's **State Capitol Museum**. Built in 1922, this three story house has high ceilinged rooms paneled in a variety of rich woods, and five fireplaces.

Displays include a variety of items relating the history of Washington's early government. This is a great place to learn about Olympia's 1853 designation as the capitol of Washington Territory, the state's entry into the union as the 42nd state as well as more recent governmental issues. Pioneer and Indian artifacts are also on display.

1855 Fort Borst Blockhouse

45 ♦ Early Washington pioneers built the Fort Borst blockhouse in 1855 for defense and protection against area Indians. Since the Indians here were friendly, the building was never used. You'll find this historic blockhouse in Centralia. To get there, simply take exit #82 off I-5 and follow Harrison Avenue to **Fort Borst Park**. The blockhouse was originally located on the nearby bank of the Chehalis River.

Pioneer Life Museum

46 ◆ Pioneers in Washington Territory lived a sparse existence. You can get an idea of how they lived at the **Lewis County Historical Museum** in Chehalis. This little museum includes a pioneer parlor, kitchen, school room, general store and blacksmith shop. You'll find these displays in the 1912 Burlington Northern Railroad depot at 599 NW Front Street.

The depot is listed on the National Historic Register and also contains train memorabilia. They are open year round, Tuesday thru Sunday from 9 am to 5 pm and Sundays from 1 to 5 pm. New exhibits are put on display every three months making this a nice spot to revisit.

1858 Territorial Church

47 ◆ West of Chehalis you can visit Washington's oldest territorial church. Tiny **Claquato Church** was built in 1858, just a few years after Washington Territory was formed. Close examination will reveal hand mortised and pegged doors, wide whip-sawn boards and hand forged square nails. The bronze bell was cast in Boston in 1857 and shipped to Olympia by way of Cape Horn.

Claquato Church is located 3 miles west of Chehalis, off Chivers Road. Take State Highway 6 out of Chehalis to Stearns Road. Follow this to Chivers Road and the church.

48 ♦ The historic **Jackson House** was built in 1844 and served as a stopping place for travelers using the northern spur of the Oregon Trail. This log cabin has been used as a home, inn, grocery store, post office and the first US District Court north of the Columbia River. Its most famous visitor was Ulysses S. Grant.

1844 Jackson House

The cabin was built by John Jackson in 1844 as a family home and was the first American settlement north of the Columbia River. The inside of the cabin can only be toured by appointment; call (206) 864-2643. Most visitors simply peer in the windows. It is furnished with a spinning wheel, simple desk, chairs, braided rug and a sharpening wheel, much as it might have been during its early years. A bed can be seen up in the loft.

The cabin is located near Marys Corner which can be reached off I-5. Signs will direct you from there.

Cowlitz County History

49 ♦ The first thing you see upon entering the **Cowlitz County Historical Museum** is an 1884 log cabin. It sort of sets the tone for your visit. Pioneer furnishings, early logging equipment, Oregon Trail memorabilia and artifacts from two local Indian tribes are also on display. I was enchanted with the items made by the Cowlitz and Chinook Indians.

You'll find this charming little museum at 405 Allen Street in Kelso. Hours are 9 am to 5 pm Tuesday thru Saturday and 1 to 5 pm on Sundays.

1876 Grist Mill

50 ♦ East of Woodland you can view what is thought to be the oldest grist mill still standing in the state of Washington. The **Cedar Creek Grist Mill** is being carefully restored. Known as the Red Bird Mill in 1876, this original operation was shut down after just 3 years. Volunteers are working hard to restore the mill to its original state. The work is done with broad axes and adzes, wooden pegs, and hand peeled studs. The Friends of the Cedar Creek Grist Mill get most of the credit.

History buffs, photographers and artists will find this 1876 mill quaint and picturesque. The building is listed on the National Register of Historic Places and located 10 miles east of Woodland on County Road 16.

The Hudson Bay Company's Fort Vancouver

51 ♦ Fort Vancouver was founded by the Hudson Bay Company in 1824 as a fur-trading post and supply depot. For the next 20 years it was the most important settlement in the Pacific Northwest. Fort Vancouver is now part of the National Park system and archaeological digs have resulted in nearly one million artifacts relating the fort's past.

A visitors center, full size reconstructed fort and informative displays and activities make this a wonderful place to spend the afternoon. The fort is open weekends from 9 am to 4 pm Labor Day thru March, and between April and Labor Day from 9 am to 5 pm daily. To reach the **Fort Vancouver National Historic Site** take the Mill Plain Boulevard east off I-5 at Vancouver and follow the signs.

Officers' Row consists of 10 houses and 11 duplexes facing the old Fort Vancouver parade grounds. The oldest is the Grant House, built in 1849, at 1106 East Evergreen Boulevard. It is the only one open to the public but has a small admission charge. The other buildings along Officers' Row were built between 1867 and 1906 and can only be viewed from the street.

The original Fort Vancouver location is marked at Grand Boulevard and East Sixth Street. You will also find an old apple tree near the intersection of I-5 and State Highway 14. It is believed to be the oldest living thing planted by man, west of the Rocky Mountains, and was planted about 1829. The **Fisher Cemetery**, 16th and Evergreen Highway, was first opened in 1851.

Antique Dolls and Railroad Artifacts

52 ◆ Vancouver's **Clark County Historical Museum** is really fun! Housed in the town's **1909 Carnegie Library Building**, it's packed with treasures. I was fascinated by the candle illuminated slide projector and the large collection of railroad memorabilia.

You'll also find an 1890 country store, pioneer kitchen and antique dolls plus lots of Indian and pioneer memorabilia. Besides the permanent displays, they offer new exhibits every few months. I once stopped by to find an extensive collection of antique dolls; it was the largest collection I'd ever seen in the Northwest. Hours are 1 to 5 pm Tuesday thru Sunday. The museum is located at 1511 Main Street.

World's Largest Rosary Collection

53 ◆ You'll find nearly 4,000 rosaries, from all over the world, at the **Skamania County Historical Society Museum** in Stevenson. The rosaries are made from a variety of materials including bones, bullets, gemstones, seeds and coins. Some are small enough to fit your ring finger; others are up to 16' in length. Many once belonged to famous people. The oldest rosary displayed was made in Bavaria in 1770. Prayer beads used by other religious groups are also included in the exhibit.

This museum also contains Cascade Indian artifacts, pioneer relics, antique musical instruments and county historical memorabilia. Outside you'll find an old Corliss Steam Engine, an early railroad caboose and other large items.

The museum is open Sundays from 1 to 6 pm year round. They are also open Monday thru Saturday from 12 to 5 pm during the summer and Thursday thru Saturday the rest of the year.

19th Century Log Flume

54 ♦ In recent years log flume rides have become popular additions to amusement parks. For most people that's as close as they'll ever come to seeing a real log flume. Visitors to the Cook area can see what was once the **world's longest log flume** in operation.

Flumes like this were popular between 1870 and 1930. This one was in operation until the 1980s. It began at the Broughton Lumber Company Mill in Willard, and carried logs down 9 miles of hillside to the Columbia River. The flume is visible along State Highway 14, near Underwood.

Ancient Indian Rock Paintings

55 ♦ The Pacific Northwest's Native Americans left lots of wonderful rock drawings along the Columbia River, but the building of dams and civilization has caused much of it to disappear.

At **Horsethief Lake State Park** you'll find a large collection of Indian pictographs. The easy trail west of the first boat ramp will lead you past some of the best. The park is located along State Highway 14, about 2 miles east of its junction with US Highway 197. You'll find additional paintings near Wishram, as well as some prehistoric stone fences.

56 ♦ Just west of Yakima we discovered another great collection of Indian paintings. My daughter likes to refer to this spot as french fry rocks since that's just what the rock formations look like. The artwork appears at all levels along this unusual spot. To find it head west of Yakima on US Highway 12 to the Power House Road exit. The paintings are south/southwest of here, near the stop sign, and are clearly marked.

1856 Fort Simcoe

57 ♦ Historic Fort Simcoe served as advance post for the Ninth Regiment infantry unit from 1856 to 1859. It was one of only two regular Army posts in the interior Washington Territory; the other was Fort Walla Walla. Five of the original fort buildings still stand. They frame the 420 square-foot parade ground and include the commanding officer's house and a squared-log blockhouse. Ongoing restorations, and a small museum where you can learn all about the history of Fort Simcoe and the Yakima Indians, make this a fun place to visit. If you'd like to tour the buildings call (206) 874-2372.

The **Fort Simcoe Historical State Park** covers 200 acres and is open daily, year round. It's located west of Toppenish; just follow State Highway 220 past the town of White Swan.

Pioneer Homestead Exhibit

58 ♦ The **Benton County Historical Museum** is a wonderful place to learn about Eastern Washington's early pioneers. It includes a recreated general store, pioneer school, 1900s parlor and a turn-of-the-century homestead shack. Pioneer quilts, dresses from the 1800s, antique dolls, an 1867 square grand piano and other antique furnishings are among the treasures on display. The museum is open Tuesday thru Saturday from 10 am to 4 pm and Sundays from 1 to 5 pm. You'll find it in Prosser, at the city park.

Historic Ellensburg

59 ♦ On July 4, 1889 more than 200 Victorian homes and 10 blocks of the downtown Ellensburg business area were consumed by fire. This tragedy dashed all hopes Ellensburg had of becoming the state capitol. The **Lynch Block Building** at Fifth and Pearl is the only existing structure to survive the fire. When it was built in 1888, the glass panes for the front windows were the largest ever brought to Central Washington.

The rebuilding of Ellensburg began that same year, less than 10 days after the fire. Most of these 1889 buildings include elaborate metal decorations and cornices. Buildings erected downtown that year include several on Third, Fourth and Pearl Streets.

The **1890 Masonic Temple** on Sixth at Pearl has large, locally made iron columns. The **1908 Fitterer Building** at Fourth and Main is a good example of early 20th century commercial architecture with metal rosettes, brick cornice work and small arched windows. The **1909 railroad depot**, on West Third, sports truncated gables with rounded arches. The interior has Tiffany tile, wainscoting, Tennessee marble, oak and nickel trim.

Central Washington University's **Barge Hall** was built in 1893. This four story Romanesque structure has two towers, red brick sandstone borders and tin and metal ornamentation. It serves as a reminder of the university's early beginnings as a normal school. The University also has a fine **Anthropology Museum**. You'll find it in the Instructional Building at 14th and D Streets. It is open during normal school hours.

The **Kittitas County Historical Museum**, at Third and Pine, is a great place to learn about Ellensburg's early history. Displays include pioneer items, Indian artifacts, antique hats and dolls plus an extensive gem collection. The museum is open weekdays from 1 to 5 pm and Saturdays from 1 to 4 pm.

1875 Olmstead Homestead

60 ◆ You can visit one of Kittitas Valley's first homesteads, an 1875 log cabin, at **Olmstead Place State Park** east of Ellensburg. The cabin, which was considered large for that time, is built of cottonwood logs squared with a broad axe. The boards were cut with a whip saw, dovetailed, and held together with round pegs cut from branches. The windows still contain the original glass which was hauled by wagon from The Dalles, Oregon. It is furnished much as it would have been when built.

Seaton School House

Other buildings were added to the homestead over the years. By 1900 it had a dairy barn, granary, wagon shed and tool house. The larger barn was added in 1909 and a milk house in 1920. The **Seaton School House** was constructed in the 1870s; the wood floor was added later. It was originally used as a home. You'll also find a huge collection of antique farm machinery and equipment here.

To reach the park, take the Kittitas exit off I-90 and drive 3 miles west. It is open weekdays throughout the spring and summer from 6:30 am to 10 pm, weekends and holidays from 1 to 4 pm. Throughout the winter and fall they are open weekdays only from 8 a.m to 5 pm. To tour the buildings call (509) 925-1943.

20 Million Year Old Petrified Forest

61 ◆ At **Ginkgo Petrified Forest State Park** you can hike along a prehistoric lake bed where 20 million year old logs can be seen in petrified form. This land, near Vantage, was once lush with trees and ferns. When the Cascade Mountain Range pushed its way upward, it stopped the moist air and caused life to spring more slowly. Lava flows covered the lake, preserving more than 200 different species of trees.

Early settlers discovered this site in 1931, but Native Americans used its petrified wood for arrowheads and

Indian petroglyphs - Ginkgo Petrified Forest State Park

trinkets long before that. At one time, more than 300 petroglyphs existed less than a mile from the current park site. Most were buried under Wanapum Reservoir, but a few have been placed on display near the Interpretive Center.

You can visit the center from mid-May thru mid-September; call (509) 856-2700 for current hours. The slide show is a must as it explains the changes the area has undergone. Samples of the many different kinds of petrified wood are also on display.

Extensive Indian Artifact Collection

62 ♦ In Moses Lake you can visit one of the state's largest collections of Indian artifacts. The **Adam East Museum** has a great number of items once belonging to local basin area tribes. Prehistoric animal bones and fossils from the famed Lind Coulee digs are also on display. This is a great place to learn about the region's prehistoric beginnings.

The museum is open from 10 am to 5 pm May thru August and 2 to 5 pm during March, April, September and October. It is located in the Moses Lake Civic Center at Fifth and Balsam.

A Coal Mining Town Gone Hollywood

63 ♦ The coal fields surrounding Roslyn were once the most extensive on the West Coast. Mining of those fields began during the 1880s and continued for 80 years. Roslyn has changed little since it was first built.

If you find it looks familiar to you, that's because it's been discovered by Hollywood. It was the site of the movie The Runner Stumbles and now tv's Northern Exposure. If you visit at the right time, you may even be there when the film crew for Northern Exposure is shooting a new episode.

I found the **Roslyn Historical Museum** a real treat! It's literally packed with relics. Organs, lamps, household artifacts, mining tools, pioneer goods and tons of miscellaneous items from times past clutter the building from floor to ceiling. Although the museum is not a large one, a person could spend hours browsing through the collection. Outside you'll find some old coal cars from one of the local mines.

The museum is open year round from 1 to 5 pm. If this doesn't match your schedule call (509) 649-2776 and the curator will try to accommodate you.

The **Roslyn Cemeteries** are clustered on a mountainside just west of town. At one time this small town had 25 separate ethnic, religious and fraternal cemeteries representing the pioneer families' diverse cultures. Many of the graves are above ground and most headstones are ornate; some even include a photograph of the deceased. To reach the cemeteries, head west on Pennsylvania or Arizona Avenue.

Telephone History and Early Cle Elum

64 ♦ The **Cle Elum Historical Museum** is always popular with children. Located in the old telephone company building, it's filled with displays showing the evolution of the telephone. Museum displays show telephone equipment from 1901 to 1987. Crank-type phones, switchboards, operator stations and every improvement right up to the automatic dialing system are included. This is the most complete telephone museum west of the Mississippi and includes hands-on exhibits. Displays depicting Cle Elum's colorful history are also found there.

The museum is at 221 E. First Street. Throughout the summer it is open Saturday thru Monday from 12 to 4 pm, Tuesday thru Friday 9 am to 4 pm. During the winter you can generally find someone there on Tuesdays between 9 am and 4 pm and Wednesday thru Friday from 9 am to 12 pm.

Cle Elum is also the site of the **Carpenter Museum**. This lovely 1914 mansion has been refurbished to its original grandeur. You can tour all three floors, including the grand ballroom that fills the entire third floor.

Most of the original furniture, including Tiffany lamps, brass beds, marble topped tables, a French victrola, Copper washing machine, oak dining table with 11 matching leaves, sleigh bedroom set, mahogany Chippendale desk, and an upright rosewood piano, fill its rooms. The house is open to the public summer weekends between 12 and 4 pm..

1880s Gold Rush Village

65 ♦ **Liberty** is a gold town that never gave up. First called Williams Creek in 1880, it was renamed

Meaghersville in 1897 after the man who first discovered gold here. Meanwhile, about 1893, a small town was being built downstream and called Liberty. By 1916 the second town was nearly empty and Meaghersville took its name.

This tiny town once sported hotels, saloons, dance halls, a general store, post office, barber shop, doctor's office, sawmill, assay office and a logging company. Once part of a collection of gold mining towns known as the Swauk Mining District, Liberty is one of the last. This is not a ghost town; it still has a few residents. It's definitely a colorful place to stop; the residents have gone out of their way to make visitors feel welcome.

One of Liberty's old buildings

Liberty can be reached by following US Highway 97 north of its junction with State Highway 970 for 3 miles. From there, follow the signs. Liberty is located 2 miles east of the highway.

66 ♦ Another piece of gold mining history can be viewed north of Liberty. The **Blewett Arrastra** was built in 1861, at a time when 260 miners worked here, and it remained active until 1880. This area was heavily populated from the 1840s to the 1880s when large chunks of gold-bearing ore were mined. This arrastra broke up those large chunks of ore into a powder, using a water wheel to move heavy drag stones across the stone base. The gold was then recovered by amalgamation with mercury.

The base of the arrastra is all that remains here, beside the creek that powered it. A historical marker along the highway, beside a large parking area, tells some of the history. Then it's just a quick trip across the highway to see the arrastra stone. Few visitors can resist the urge to inspect the creek's bed for gold-bearing rocks. You'll find this historic treasure near milepost #174 on US Highway 97, 11 miles south of US Highway 2.

Authentic Pioneer Village

67 ♦ The collection of Indian artifacts and pioneer relics at the **Chelan County Historical Society Museum** ranks among the top five in the nation. Displays include a pioneer village containing 16 historic cabins furnished to depict life here in the 1880s.

You can visit a one-room log school built in 1886 and an 1872 post office. The assay office was built in 1879 and includes a mine portal replica with timbers, track and ore cars from the Blewett mines. The 1872 Horan cabin, 1888 Richardson cabin and 1891 Weythman cabin have all been restored and are furnished much like they would have been when first built. A barber shop, general store, millinery shop, jail, doctor-dentist office, saloon, blacksmith shop, print shop, mission, railroad depot and 1891 waterwheel are also found within the village.

Pioneer village - Chelan County Historical Society Museum

The museum is open to the public from April thru October. Monday thru Saturday they open at 10 am and close at 4:30 pm; on Sundays they don't open until 12:30 pm. You'll find the museum complex at the east end of the Cottage Avenue Bridge, in Cashmere.

Hands-on History

68 ♦ The **North Central Washington Museum** is a great place to experience the "olden days" first hand.

Visitors can try making rope, washing and ironing clothes, churning butter and baking bread without the aid of electricity. On Mondays, at noon, they offer a pioneer program.

The museum covers two floors in the old post office building, and includes a 19th century trading post and general store, as well as exhibits on the history of aviation and a working scale model railroad. You can see a 1903 horse-drawn hook and ladder fire wagon, vintage camera collection, and a museum of miniatures as well. The museum is located at 127 S. Mission in Wenatchee. Open year round, hours are 10 am to 4 pm weekdays, 1 to 4 pm weekends. They are closed weekends during January.

Barbed Wire and Other Pioneer Exhibits

69 ◆ Inside the **Douglas County Historical Society Museum** in Waterville you'll find a variety of fascinating collections. They have one of the state's best rock collections, plus lots of petroglyphs, Indian artifacts, pioneer goods and an extensive early barbed wire display . The museum is only open during the summer. Hours are 11 am to 5 pm Wednesday thru Sunday. You'll find the museum in Waterville, on Central Avenue.

Indian Caves

70 ◆ The **Lake Lenore Caves** were used as temporary shelters by nomadic prehistoric hunters. Created when melting glaciers forced basalt chunks from the coulee walls, they are small pockets in the rocky hillside. You'll find them along State Highway 17 near Coulee City, 5 miles south of Sun Lakes State Park.

A trail leading to four of the caves has been developed near the north end of Lake Lenore. If you take the right-hand path at the Y you'll encounter the larger of the caves.

Prehistoric Giant Waterfall

71 ♦ **Dry Falls** is one of the greatest waterfalls in geologic history. It once held a flood of water 3.5 times wider and 2.5 times higher than Niagara Falls. Created during the ice age, this waterfall came to be when the Columbia River had to carve a new channel to avoid an ice dam. Although completely dry now, the falls ran heavily for 4-6,000 years and could be heard more than 100 miles away. Nearly half of the glacial floodwaters covering North America thundered through this historic river bed.

At the **Dry Falls Interpretive Center** you'll see exhibits that tell the story of the area's evolution. You'll learn about the changes that took place here in the past 20 million years and how Miocene and Pliocene lava floods, earthquakes and the ice age changed the land. Outside, a viewpoint overlooks the empty falls. Trails can be followed for closer inspection. You'll find the center southwest of Coulee City. It's open May thru mid-September; call (509) 632-5583 for current hours.

Fort Okanogan History

72 ◆ You can learn all about the region's early fur trappers at the **Fort Okanogan Interpretive Center**. It overlooks the site where John Jacob built the Pacific Fur Company in 1811. In 1821 this site became part of the Hudson Bay Company operation. Between 1831 and 1837 the fort was moved to a new site 2 miles away. Three archaeological digs done in the area have located the remains of both sites.

When Wells Dam flooded this area, everything was completely covered with water. The interpretive center offers audio-visual and pictorial displays depicting Washington's first American settlement. Exhibits include early Indian artifacts, a hand carved dug out canoe and a wonderful diorama of the fort structure. The center is 1 mile east of Brewster on US Highway 97 and open throughout the summer season.

1897 Waring Castle

73 ◆ In 1897 Waring Castle was the showplace of the Methow Valley. Today it serves as the **Shafer Museum**. On the museum grounds you can visit an 1889 homesteader cabin typical of the cabins built and lived in by area pioneers.

A 1910 log cabin, houses a turn of the century printing office. A stage coach, horse drawn sightseeing bus, fire hose cart, 1880 sleigh, 1914 Ford, early Rickenbacher automobile and an ancient Indian canoe plus numerous other interesting antiques, can be seen in the surrounding sheds and across the lawn area.

Inside the museum you'll find pioneer furniture and household items.

The museum is located in Winthrop, on Castle Avenue. It is open daily, from June 1 thru Labor Day, 9 am to 8 pm. The balance of the year they are open weekends only from 10 am to 5 pm. Winthrop has the flavor of an old west village with false front buildings, board sidewalks, hitching posts and watering troughs. You feel as though a stage coach will be racing thru town at any moment.

Downtown Winthrop

Oroville Area Ghost Towns

74 ♦ Nighthawk, Golden and Weeheesville are three old mining areas outside of Oroville. To find **Nighthawk**, head west out of town on Central Avenue. This will take you up the Similkameen Gorge, past the road to Enloe Dam, along the Similkameen River to the Nighthawk Y. Heading south at the Y, you cross the river and arrive in Nighthawk. A number of old mining sites can be found in this area.

75 ◆ To find what remains of **Golden** and **Weeheesville**, take 12th Avenue out of Oroville. At Golden Road turn right and follow the signs to the Wannacut Lake. Travel past Blue Lake and keep to your left, heading toward the lake. At the north end of the lake, where two roads meet, the mining community of Golden once sat. Continuing around the lake, take the dirt road at the lake's south end. This will lead you to the old Weeheesville townsite. This land, especially that to the west, was once peppered with gold mining claims.

76 ◆ East of Oroville about 15 miles is the town of **Molson**, a living ghost town. Many of the pioneer buildings have been preserved. The old **Molson School Museum** houses pioneer exhibits. It's open throughout the summer from 10 am to 5 pm and offers an excellent chance to learn about local pioneers and view old mining equipment. This is a great little town. The people are friendly and you'll find lots of visible history.

Curlew Lake Mining Area

77 ◆ The Curlew Lake area, north of Republic, was once an Indian settlement. Many artifacts left behind by those first inhabitants have been uncovered. Homesteaders left their mark too. Remains of old homesteads and log cabins can be seen throughout the area. A number of old mining shafts also exist, dating from a time around the turn of the century when gold mining was a popular pastime for many. To reach Curlew Lake take State Highway 21 north of Republic for 9 miles.

Eocene Fossil Site

78 ♦ At the **Stonerose Interpretive Center** you can see 50 million year old fossils. Displays contain Eocene flora and fauna including fossils of the oldest known rose and some of the best preserved upland Eocene fossils in the United States. Many of the species found at the center are extinct.

The center is located at the south end of Republic and open May thru November. Visitors are allowed to dig for fossils at the **Book Hill** site, .5 mile northwest of the center. You need to check in at the center both before and after collecting. Chisels, hammers and other equipment may be rented at the center. When you return, the folks there will identify the fossils for you. Beginners can get help with their hunt daily between 10 am and 2 pm.

Underwater City and Indian History

79 ♦ Native Americans have visited the Kettle Falls area for more than 9,000 years. The first non-Indian came here in 1811, and the Hudson Bay Company built a trading post here in 1826. They named it Fort Colville. At that time, this was the center of trade and the most important post in the northwest. By 1840 they were shipping out 18,000 furs a year.

St. Paul's Mission is one of the oldest churches still standing in the state of Washington. This rustic log chapel was built in 1847. It sits in an area where summer fishing camps and Indian burial grounds go back 9,000 years. Recent archaeological digs have established this as one of the oldest continuously occupied sites in the entire Northwest.

A trail along the bluffs west of town overlooks the original site of Fort Colville as well as the ancient Indian fishing grounds. Both were covered by water when the Columbia River was dammed by the Grand Coulee to create Lake Roosevelt.

Many Indian artifacts are on display at the **Kettle Falls Historical Center**. Exhibits illustrate why those Native Americans found this area so attractive. You'll learn about the local Indians, the important role of their Salmon Chief, how visiting tribes were treated and why they followed the seasons.

Two small towns, Kettle and Marcus, were also flooded by the rising water created by the Grand Coulee Dam. During the spring drawdown of Lake Roosevelt you can actually walk the streets of **Old Marcus**. Sidewalks, foundations and street signs remain preserved by the cold water. This rare treat can only be seen in early spring. At that time you'll find Old Marcus 5 miles north of Kettle Falls, along State Highway 25.

Farm Machinery Museum and Blacksmith Shop

80 ◆ The beautiful 7.5 acre **Keller Historical Park** in Colville includes a number of historic buildings and displays. A good place to start your tour is the **Stevens County Historical Society Museum**. Stevens County is one of the oldest and most historic areas in the state and this museum tells the tale of its historic beginnings. You'll learn about the geological history, area Indians, early industry, Fort Colville and local pioneers.

The park's handsome 1910 **Keller House** is an excellent example of elegant early 20th century architecture. This three story home, carriage house and garden are on the National Register of Historic Places. Its beautifully crafted interior is an excellent example of early twentieth century elegance with its beautiful red birch beams and woodwork. It is decorated much as it was in its early days.

The **Machinery Building** contains horse drawn and steam powered farming equipment from the early 1900s.. A Case steam traction engine, horse drawn ice cutter, side plow, covered wagon and a rare 1925 grain separator needing 23 men for operation are all on display.

The **Blacksmith Shop** is a new exhibit and furnished just as one would have been in the late 1800s. From time to time, they offer living history displays here when visitors can watch as the iron is heated and the smith works.

Several old log cabins have been moved to the park, now serving as special exhibits. The **farmstead cabin** is furnished for a family, the **trapper's cabin** has items a turn-of-the-century trapper would need and the **fire lookout tower** is just as it was when in service on Graves Mountain. **Colville's first school**

house is also here. It's logs were hand hewn with a broadaxe, squared on four sides and connected by dove-tail joints. The little school house is furnished with board benches, desks, a chalkboard and a big potbelly stove.

The park buildings are open daily from May thru September. During May they are open from 1 to 4 pm; the balance of the season, they open at 10 am Monday thru Saturday.

Indian Ceremonial Caves

81 ◆ Manresa Grotto is located on the Kalispel Indian Reservation northeast of Usk. The above-ground caves were formed by glacial activity and have long been used by Native Americans for ceremonial activities. To reach them, cross the Pend Oreille River at Usk and proceed to the reservation road. Turn north; the caves are about 8 miles down. Keep your eyes open and you may see buffalo grazing along the way.

Learn How the Settlers Made Their Living

82 ◆ Chewelah was once a gathering place for Native American tribes who came to fish, hunt game and gather the abundant roots and berries. You can learn more about those first inhabitants at the **Chewelah Museum**. Stevens County mining history, area logging, military memorabilia and pioneer tools are also on display. The museum is only open during the summer months; hours are 1 to 5 pm daily.

Steam Engines and Antique Farm Machinery

83 ♦ Newport is in both Washington and Idaho. The state line cuts through town leaving the old town portion, which was settled in the late 1800s, in Idaho. This part of town still retains a lot of its original frontier character.

A giant Corliss steam engine marks the location of the **Pend Oreille County Historical Society Museum Complex**. Exhibits include the old Milwaukee Depot, a wonderful collection of historical photographs, steamship memorabilia and lots of items used by the regions early settlers. Museum volunteers are also piecing together an authentic turn of the century village. It already includes a restored and furnished log cabin, a fascinating farm machinery display and an early day schoolhouse.

You'll find the museum where State Highway 2 meets Washington Avenue. It's only open during the summer, from 10 am to 4 pm Monday thru Saturday.

1886 Pioneer Farm

84 ♦ The **Owen Farm** has been in the same family since 1886. These fine folks have established a pioneer museum at the original homesite. The farm house is furnished much as it was in years past, but a doll collection and a room full of war artifacts are there too. An old time grocery store, barber shop, post office, log cabins, a covered wagon, and several old cars are nearby. The homestead museum is located north of Chattaroy.

They welcome visitors from Mother's Day to Labor Day from 10 am to 6 pm. To find the farm, head north out of Chattaroy and west on the Denison-Chattaroy Road. Turn north on Regail Road; the museum will be on your left.

1880 Fort Spokane

85 ♦ Fort Spokane was constructed in 1880 at the spot where the Spokane and Columbia Rivers join forces. This location was chosen as a central post for the protection of settlers along the upper Columbia River. During the next 12 years more than 45 buildings were erected. At the height of Army occupation, 300 soldiers, plus many families and civilians lived at Fort Spokane.

After the fort was abandoned in 1929, it became a popular picnic site for local residents. In 1960 Fort Spokane was transferred to the National Park Service and major restoration efforts began. Four original

Mule barn - Fort Spokane

buildings can be explored as you take a self-guided tour through the fort. The Fort Spokane ranger station is located in the 1892 brick guardhouse and is open all summer from 8 am to 6 pm. Inside you can watch a 10 minute film, view talking displays revealing fort life and visit the jail cells. Outside are the remains of root cellars and fort buildings, a mule barn and easy trails.

This historic site is just a few miles southwest of Miles and only open during the summer. You can visit between 9 am and 6 pm any day of the week. Sunday mornings are a good time to come, as you will sometimes find costumed "troops" putting on a living history demonstration.

Washington's Friendliest Museum

86 ♦ The **Lincoln County Historical Society Museum** is a delightful small town museum with lots of hands-on exhibits. The people are friendly and the

Threshing machine - Lincoln County Historical Society Museum

indoor exhibits are beautifully done, but the real treasures are out back. You can view early steam engines, an old Case threshing machine, an 1890s horse-powered hay baler, and a combine so large it took 32 horses to pull. Be sure to walk across the street for a look at the tiny 1879 log school house.

You'll find this treasure in Davenport. The museum is open Tuesday thru Sunday between 1 and 4 pm throughout the summer.

1810 Trading Post Exhibit

87 ♦ Spokane House was a Canadian-owned trading post built in 1810 and the first permanent non-Indian settlement in Washington. The trading post was abandoned in 1826. Items relating trading post and Indian history are on display at the **Spokane House Interpretive Center**. Exhibits include a detailed model of the original Spokane House, antique weapons, Indian relics and trading post memorabilia.

The center is open Wednesday thru Sunday from mid-May to the end of August; call (509) 456-3964 for current hours. It's located 9 miles northwest of Spokane, where the Spokane and Little Spokane Rivers meet. State Highway 291 will take you there.

Crosby, Hopkins & Northwest Collections

88 ♦ Gonzaga University in Spokane has a large cache of Bing Crosby memorabilia. Although the bulk of the collection is not displayed, some of the most significant items form a permanent display at the university library. The **Crosbyana Room** exhibits contain personal memorabilia, gold records and the Oscar Bing received for his performance in "Going My Way." You'll find it on the second floor. Visitors are welcome whenever the room is not in use for meetings or classes.

The **Gonzaga University library** also contains a number of other historical items. These include a collection of books brought to the Pacific Northwest by early missionaries, rare classical, philosophical and religious texts dating to the early 1400s, historic materials documenting the development of the Northwest Territories and a collection of more than 4,000 items related to the life and works of Gerald Manley Hopkins. The library is at East 502 Boone Avenue.

Historic Spokane

89 ♦ The first permanent non-Indian settlers arrived on the banks of the Spokane River in 1871, but this frontier village didn't amount to much until 1881. That was when the Northern Pacific Railroad reached Spokane. Street cars, gracious Victorian homes, a hospital, bank, water works and electric light plant soon followed. Then disaster struck. In 1889 most of downtown Spokane was destroyed by fire. The **Crescent Building** at West 913-925 Riverside was the only block left standing.

The **Review Building** at West 927 Riverside was built in 1890 and is listed in the National Register of Historic Places. The **Spokane County Courthouse**,

West 1116 Broadway, is a French Renaissance building with impressive towers and turrets. It was built in 1894.

A number of lovely older homes exist in Spokane. These are private homes and can only be viewed from the street. Some of the most impressive are as follows. On West First Street - 2340 (1898), 2328 (1898), 2316 (1898), 2123 (1900), 1923 (1890) and 1725 (1881). On West Seventh Street - 507 (1898), 701 (1897) and 815 (1898).

The Cathedral of St. John the Evangelist was begun in 1925. Located at East 127 12th Avenue, it is English Gothic in design. The exterior stone was quarried near Tacoma. The elaborately carved west entrance leads to an area tiled in Pewabic pottery with 2 stained glass windows. The first depicts the landing of the pilgrims in New England, the second a 19th century midwest church. Many other stained glass windows grace the cathedral as well. The ceiling too is a thing of beauty and the carillon holds 49 cast bells. The largest weighs nearly 5,000 pounds, the smallest 17 pounds.

Although you can see the church anytime it's open, you'll learn more about this elegant building if you take one of the guided tours. Volunteer guides are at the cathedral from 12 to 3 pm on Tuesday, Thursday and Saturday. Donations are welcome.

You can visit Spokane's original crossroads, **Four Corners**, at the intersection of Spokane Falls Boulevard and Howard Street. This was where the Glovers, the town's first family, operated their store.

It's also the site of the old railroad yard which now serves as a **historic park**. From there you can see the old **Great Northern Depot Clock Tower** which is all that remains of the city's 1902 station. When built, it was considered to be the finest west of Chicago. The **1896 Flour Mill** has been converted to hold shops and restaurants.

1890 Ritzville

90 ♦ The Burlington Northern Railroad Depot and the **1890 Burroughs Home** are two notable buildings found in downtown Ritzville. The latter also serves as the town museum.

The **Burrows Home Museum** is open from May to September and a sign outside lists phone numbers to call for access at other times of the year. Small-town museums like this one provide a terrific opportunity to learn about early Washington history. This one will show you who the town founders were and other historical facts about Ritzville.

The Ritzville **Carnegie Library** is listed on the National Register of Historic Places. This building was finished in 1907 and houses much of the area's historic memorabilia as well as the town's book collection. Ritzville is such a small town, you'll need no directions to find this and other historic buildings.

1874 Pioneer Cabin

91 ♦ The **Perkins House** was built in the mid 1880s by James Perkins, a Whitman County pioneer and the founder of Colfax. Victorian in style, the home has three ground level porches and a number of balcony porches. The interior has been restored and refurbished in an authentic turn-of-the-century manner. The house is located in northwest Colfax, on Perkins Avenue. It is open to the public, June thru August on Thursday and Sunday afternoons between 1 and 5 pm.

Perkins House

Out back you'll find the city's first house, the **Perkins Cabin**. It was built in 1874. Its rough-cut timber construction is covered with white-washed boards that suggest the austere lifestyle encountered by early area pioneers.

An Outstanding Collection of Museums

92 ♦ Washington State University, in Pullman, is a gold mine of fascinating museums, collections and exhibits. They are open weekdays only, during the school year. The **Anthropology Museum** has exhibits covering the evolution of humans, their tools, products, language development and cultures. Located in College Hall, it is open 10 am to 4 pm.

The **Conner Museum** contains more than 700 Northwest birds and mammals. Stuffed specimens include moose, caribou, deer, antelope, bighorn sheep, mountain goats, bear, coyote and cougar. Many of the exhibits were once part of Washington's 1894 World Fair. Live reptiles, amphibians and fish inhabit the large terraria. The museum is in Science Hall and open 8 am to 5 pm.

The **Ownbey Herbarium** in Heald Hall is one of the best in the US. Founded in 1890, it contains hundreds of specimens of flowering plants, ferns, gymnosperms, mosses, liverworts and lichens. Both are open 8:30 am to 5 pm. The **Mycological Herbarium** in Johnson Hall has more than 70,000 specimens of fungi and is the largest collection of its kind west of the Mississippi. It is shown by appointment only.

The **Geology Museum**, room 124 of the Physical Science Building, includes an outstanding petrified wood collection. It also contains a great display of fluorescent rocks. Other rock and mineral collections can be viewed throughout the building. The best times to see these exhibits is between 8 am and 5 pm.

Heritage House, located between the Owen Library and Cleveland Hall, is a Black cultural center. In the foyer you will find a permanent collection of artifacts relevant to Black history and achievements. Oriental art is the theme of White Hall's **Drucker Collection**. Hand crafted chests, ornate furniture, oriental rugs, a hand woven tapestry of silk and gold, fine porcelain, brass and jade artifacts and antiques from the Orient are all on display.

Other campus museums include the **Veterinary Anatomy Museum** in Wegner Hall, **Museum of Art** in the Fine Arts Center and a large **insect collection** in room 385 of Johnson Hall.

Turn-of-the-century Village

93 ♦ Asotin is not a typical tourist stop, but a sleepy little village built prior to the turn of the century. Historic features include gracious turn-of-the-century homes, an 1884 jail and stockade, an aged flour mill and a memorial bridge. Asotin was built at the historic site of the Nez Perce Indians' winter camp.

The town is situated at the junction of Asotin Creek and the Snake River in the state's southwest corner. It was here that area Indians came to hide from the snow, feeding their families on the bountiful fish and wildlife. **Indian rock paintings** can be seen at Buffalo Eddy, south of town, as well as an area about 15 miles north of town along State Highway 129.

The **Asotin County Historical Museum** is located at Third and Filmore, in a 1920 building that once served as a funeral parlor. April thru October the museum is open 12 to 5 pm Tuesday thru Saturday. Winter hours are Friday 1 to 5 pm and Saturday 9 am to 5 pm.

Historic Dayton

94 ♦ The **Dayton Depot** is the oldest railroad station in the state of Washington. It was built in 1881 and moved to its present location, 222 Commercial Street, in 1899. The depot was in use until 1974 and

Dayton Depot

is listed in the National Register of Historic Places. It's open to the public from early June thru Labor Day, Tuesday thru Saturday, between 1 and 5 pm.

Dayton is a picturesque little town full of 19th century brick buildings. This county seat was first homesteaded in 1859. The **Columbia County Courthouse**, on Main Street, was built in 1886 and is the oldest in the state still in daily use. It's open weekdays only between 8:30 am and 5 pm.

Other historic buildings can be seen on East Clay and Oak as well as South Second, Third and Fourth. Most are private homes and can only be viewed from the street. Many were built between 1871 and the turn of the century.

Sacajawea's Part in Northwest History

95 ♦ When Sacajawea joined the Lewis and Clark Expedition she was a new mother and not yet twenty. Her son had been born just weeks before the group headed west. The young woman was a great asset to the expedition; in fact many believe the journey would never have been completed had she not helped them purchase horses from the Shoshonis for the treacherous crossing of the Rocky Mountains.

At the **Sacajawea Interpretive Center** you can learn all about this brave young woman and her role in the famous Lewis and Clark Expedition.

The center also has a wonderful collection of Indian artifacts. You'll find stone hammers, bone pipes and a myriad of tools and utensils made by Columbia Basin prehistoric tribes. Displays show how the tools were made and used. It's all located in **Sacajawea State Park** at the junction of the Columbia and Snake Rivers, southeast of Pasco. The center is open from May thru September; call (509) 545-2361 for current hours.

Pasco is also the site of the **Franklin County Historical Museum**. This is a great place to learn how the region's homesteaders survived. Displays include historic photos, early carpentry and farming tools, antique furnishings, toys and dolls. The railroad memorabilia and a 1910 fashion display were our favorites. The museum is located at 305 N. Fourth and open 12 to 4 pm, Tuesday thru Saturday.

Washington's Oldest City

96 ♦ The Walla Walla area was settled by white missionaries in 1836, when Marcus and Narcissa Whitman founded the Whitman Mission. Walla Walla grew out of this effort and is Washington's oldest city. Main Street was built along an old Indian Trail.

Stately old brick buildings line Walla Walla's downtown streets. At First and Main you'll find the **1890 Bee Hive Building**. Across Main, the **Barrett Building**, with its ornate upper stories, was built in 1882. The **1879 hotel building** at Second and Main is also interesting.

If you follow Main down to Fourth Street you'll find two especially ornate buildings on opposite corners. The first, the **1880 Whitman-Lacey Building**, sports cast-iron relief pillars. The **Dacres Hotel**, built in 1899, has two entirely different facades. Both are spectacular.

Indian Massacre Site

97 ♦ The **Whitman Mission** was an important stop along the Oregon Trail in the 1830s. Today it is one of Washington's National Historic Sites. The mission at Waiilatpu was founded among the Cayuse Indians in 1836 by Marcus and Narcissa Whitman. After 11 years of working with the Indians, the mission effort ended in violence. On November 29, 1847, a band of Cayuse attacked the mission and killed Marcus Whitman, his wife and 16 others. Nearly 50 more were taken captive.

Whitman Mission display

At the mission site, you can take a self-guided tour of the grounds. You'll find several audio stations where you can listen to the story of the Whitmans and their contribution to the development of the Pacific Northwest. There is also a covered wagon, Indian teepee and trails for exploring at the site. There is a small charge to go inside the visitors center; children are admitted free. To reach the Whitman Mission, follow State Highway 11 south of Walla Walla 7 miles.

IMPORTANT ADDRESSES

You'll find a wealth of information available at tourism information centers throughout Oregon and Washington. Write or call them before planning your trip. Many have 800 numbers for out of state calls. Ask for listings of hotels, restaurants and local attractions. Stop by when in the area too, it's a great way to learn about regional specialties.

State Tourism Information Centers:

Oregon Tourism Division
775 Summer Street, N.E.
Salem, OR 97310
(800) 547-7842 or (800) 233-3306 in OR

Washington State
Tourism Development Division
General Admin. Building
Olympia, WA 98504-0613
(206) 586-2088 or 586-2102

Oregon Tourism Information Centers:

Albany Visitors Assn.
P.O. Box 965
300 Second Avenue S.W.
Albany, OR 97321
928-0911 or (800) 526-2256

Baker County Visitors/Conv.
Bureau
490 Campbell Street
Baker City, OR 97814
523-3356 or (800) 523-1235

Ashland Chamber of
Commerce
P.O. Box 1360
110 E. Main
Ashland, OR 97520
(503) 482-3486

Bay Area Chamber of
Commerce
P.O. Box 210
50 E. Central
Coos Bay, OR 97420
269-0215 or (800) 824-8486

Astoria Area Chamber of
Commerce
P.O. Box 176
111 Marine Drive
Astoria, OR 97103
(503) 325-6311

Bend Chamber of Commerce
Visitors Center
63085 N. Highway 97
Bend, OR 97701
(503) 382-3221

Brookings-Harbor Chamber of
Commerce
P.O. Box 940
Highway 101/South-Harbor
Brookings, OR 97415
(503) 469-3181

Cannon Beach Chamber of
Commerce
P.O. Box 64
Second & Spruce
Cannon Beach, OR 97110
(503) 436-2623

Cascade Locks Visitor Center
P.O. Box 307
Marine Park Drive
Cascade Locks, OR 97014
(503) 374-8619

Central Oregon Visitors Center
63085 N. Highway 97
Bend, OR 97701
(503) 382-3221

Corvallis Visitors/Conv.
Bureau
420 NW 2nd
Corvallis, OR 97330
757-1544 or (800) 334-8118

Cottage Grove Chamber of
Commerce
P.O. Box 587
710 Row River Road
Cottage Grove, OR 97424
(503) 942-2411

Depoe Bay Chamber of
Commerce
P.O. Box 21
630 S.E. Highway 101
Depoe Bay, OR 97341
(503) 765-2889

Eugene-Springfield
Visitors/Conv. Bureau
P.O. Box 10286
305 W. Seventh
Eugene, OR 97440
484-5307 or (800) 547-5445

Florence Area Chamber of
Commerce
P.O. Box 26000
270 Highway 101
Florence, OR 97439
(503) 997-3128

Forest Grove Chamber of
Commerce
2417 Pacific Avenue
Forest Grove, OR 97116
(503) 357-3006

Gold Beach Chamber of
Commerce
Box 3
1225 S. Ellensburg
Gold Beach, OR 97444
247-7526 or (800) 525-2334

Grant County Chamber of
Commerce
281 W. Main
John Day, OR 97845
(503) 575-0547

Grants Pass-Josephine County
Chamber of Commerce
P.O. Box 970
1501 N.E. Sixth Street
Grants Pass, OR 97526
476-7717 or (800) 547-5927

Harney County Chamber of
Commerce
18 West D Street
Burns, OR 97720
(503) 573-2636

Heppner Chamber of
Commerce
P.O. Box 1232
289 N. Main
Heppner, OR 97836
(503) 676-5536

Greater Hermiston Chamber of
Commerce
P.O. Box 185
540 S. Highway 395
Hermiston, OR 97838
(503) 567-6151

Hood River County Chamber of
Commerce
Port Marina Park
Hood River, OR 97031
386-2000 or (800) 366-3530

Jacksonville Chamber of
Commerce
P.O. Box 33
185 N. Oregon Street
Jacksonville, OR 97530
(503) 899-8118

Klamath County Tourism
P.O. Box 1867
Klamath County Museum
Building
Klamath Falls, OR 97601
884-0666 or (800) 445-6728

La Grande-Union County
Chamber of Commerce
2111 Adams
La Grande, OR 97850
963-8588 or (800) 848-9969

LaPine Chamber of Commerce
P.O. Box 616
LaPine, OR 97739
(503) 536-9771

Lake County Chamber of
Commerce
513 Center Street
Lakeview, OR 97630
(503) 947-6040

Lincoln City Visitors/Conv.
Center
P.O. Box 109
801 S.W. Highway 101
Lincoln City, OR 97367
994-2164 or (800) 452-2151

Lower Umpqua Chamber of
Commerce
P.O. Box 11
Highway 101 & Highway 38
Reedsport, OR 97467
(503) 271-3495

Mt. Hood Visitors Information
Center
P.O. Box 342
65000 E. Highway 26
Welches, OR 97067
(503) 622-4822

Madras-Jefferson County
Chamber of Commerce
P.O. Box 770
197 S.E. Fifth Street
Madras, OR 97741
(503) 475-2350 or 475-6975

McKenzie River Chamber of
Commerce
P.O. Box 1117
Leaburg, OR 97489
(503) 896-3330

McMinnville Chamber of
Commerce
417 N. Adams
McMinnville, OR 97128
(503) 472-6196

Greater Medford
Visitors/Conv. Bureau
304 S. Central
Medford, OR 97501
(503) 779-4847

Monmouth-Independence Area
Chamber of Commerce
P.O. Box 401
110 N. Atwater
Monmouth, OR 97361
838-4268 or (800) 772-2806

Myrtle Point Chamber of
Commerce
P.O. Box 265
424 Fifth Street
Myrtle Point, OR 97458
(503) 572-2626

Newberg Area Chamber of
Commerce
115 N. Washington
Newberg, OR 97132
(503) 538-2014

Greater Newport Chamber of
Commerce
555 S.W. Coast Highway
Newport, OR 97365
265-8801 or (800) 262-7844

North Bend Info. Center
P.O. Box B
1380 Sherman
North Bend, OR 97459
756-4613 or (800) 824-8486

North Santian Chamber of
Commerce
815 N.W. Santiam Blvd.
Mill City, OR 97360
(503) 897-2865

Nyssa Chamber of Commerce
212 Main Street
Nyssa, OR 97913
(503) 372-3091

Oakridge-Westfir Chamber of
Commerce
P.O. Box 217
48711 Highway 58
Oakridge, OR 97463
(503) 782-4146

Ontario Chamber of Commerce
88 S.W. Third Avenue
Ontario, OR 97914
(503) 889-8012

Oregon City Chamber of
Commerce
500 Abernethy Road
Oregon City, OR 97045
(503) 656-1619

Pendleton Chamber of
Commerce
25 SE Dorion
Pendleton, OR 97801
276-7411 or (800) 452-9403 in
OR, (800) 547-8911 USA

Philomath Area Chamber of
Commerce
P.O. Box 606
1604 Main Street
Philomath, OR 97370
(503) 929-2454

Port Orford Chamber of
Commerce
P.O. Box 637
Highway 101
Port Orford, OR 97465
(503) 332-8055

Portland/Oregon Visitors
Association
26 S.W. Salmon
Portland, OR 97204
222-2223 or (800) 345-3214

Prineville-Crook County
Chamber of Commerce
P.O. Box 546
390 N. Fairview
Prineville, OR 97754
(503) 447-6304

Redmond Chamber of
Commerce
106 S.W. Seventh
Redmond, OR 97756
(503) 548-5191 or 923-5191

Rogue River Chamber of
Commerce
P.O. Box 457
Rogue River, OR 97537
(503) 582-0242

Roseburg Visitors/Conv.
Bureau
P.O. Box 1262
410 S.E. Spruce
Roseburg, OR 97470
672-9731 or (800) 444-9584

St. Helens Chamber of
Commerce
174 N. Columbia River
Highway
St. Helens, OR 97051
(503) 397-0685

Salem Convention & Visitors
Assn.
1313 Mill Street S.E.
Salem, OR 97301
581-4325 or (800) 874-7012

Seaside Chamber of Commerce
P.O. Box 7
7 N. Roosevelt
Seaside, OR 97138
738-6391 or (800) 444-6740

Silverton Area Chamber of
Commerce
P.O. Box 257
306 S. Water
Silverton, OR 97381
(503) 873-5615

Springfield Area Chamber of
Commerce
P.O. Box 155
101 South A Street
Springfield, OR 97477
(503) 746-1651

Sunriver Area Chamber of
Commerce
P.O. Box 3246
Village Mall - Building 12
Sunriver, OR 97707
(503) 593-8149

Sweet Home Chamber of
Commerce
1575 Main Street
Sweet Home, OR 97386
(503) 367-6186

The Dalles Visitors/Conv.
Bureau
901 E. Second Street
The Dalles, OR 97058
296-6616 or (800) 255-3385

Tillamook Chamber of
Commerce
3705 Highway 101 North
Tillamook, OR 97141
(503) 842-7525

Umatilla Chamber of
Commerce
P.O. Box 59
1300 Sixth Street #A
Umatilla, OR 97882
922-4825 or (800) 542-4944

Waldport Chamber of
Commerce
P.O. Box 669
Highway 101 & Spring Street
Waldport, OR 97394
(503) 563-2133

Wallowa County Chamber of
Commerce
P.O. Box 427
107 S.W. First
Enterprise, OR 97828
(503) 426-4622

Washington County Visitors
Assn.
10172 S.W. Washington
Square Rd.
Tigard, OR 97223
684-5555 or (800) 537-3149

Yachats Area Chamber of
Commerce
P.O. Box 728
441 Highway 101
Yachats, OR 97498
(503) 547-3530

Washington Tourism Information Centers:

Anacortes Chamber of
Commerce
1319 Commercial
Anacortes, WA 98221
(206) 293-3832

Bainbridge Island Chamber of
Commerce
153 Madrone Lane N.
Winslow, WA 98110
(206) 842-3700

Bellingham/Whatcom County
Visitors/Conv. Bureau
904 Potter Street
Bellingham, WA 98226
(206) 671-3990

Blaine Chamber of Commerce
P.O. Box Q
900 Peace Portal Drive
Blaine, WA 98230
(206) 332-4544

Bremerton/Kitsap County
Visitors/Conv. Bureau
120 Washington Avenue #101
Bremerton, WA 98310
(206) 479-3588

Chewelah Chamber of
Commerce
P.O. Box 94
110 E. Main Street
Chewelah, WA 99109
(509) 935-8991

Clallam Bay-Sekiu Chamber of
Commerce
Highway 112 Downtown
Clallam Bay, WA 98326
(206) 963-2339

Cle Elum Chamber of
Commerce
P.O. Box 43
221 E. First Street
Cle Elum, WA 98922
(509) 674-5958

Colfax Chamber of Commerce
P.O. Box 166
N. 612 Main Street
Colfax, WA 99111
(509) 397-3712

Colville Chamber of Commerce
P.O. Box 267
309 S. Main
Colville, WA 99114
(509) 684-5973

Davenport Chamber of
Commerce
P.O. Box 869
Seventh & Park
Davenport, WA 99122
(509) 725-6711

East King County
Visitors/Conv. Bureau
515 116th Avenue N.E. #111
Bellevue, WA 98004
(206) 455-1926

Edmonds Chamber of
Commerce
Fifth & Bell Streets
Edmonds, WA 98020
(206) 776-6711

Ellensburg Chamber of
Commerce
436 N. Sprague
Ellensburg, WA 98926
(509) 925-3137

Ferndale Chamber of
Commerce
5640 Riverside Drive
Ferndale, WA 98248
(206) 384-3042

Forks Chamber of Commerce
P.O. Box 1249
U.S. Highway 101 @ Airport
Forks, WA 98331

Grand Coulee Dam Area
Chamber of Commerce
P.O. Box 760
306 Midway
Grand Coulee, WA 99133

Kelso Chamber of Commerce
105 Minor Road (Exit #39)
Kelso, WA 98626
(206) 577-8058

Kettle Falls Chamber of
Commerce
P.O. Box 276
205 E. Third/Highway 395
Kettle Falls, WA 99141

Klickitat County Visitor Center
Maryhill Highway @ Bridge
Goldendale, WA 98620
(509) 773-4395

La Conner Chamber of
Commerce
P.O. Box 644
Lime Dock Blvd @ First Street
La Conner, WA 98257
(206) 466-4778

Lake Chelan Chamber of
Commerce
P.O. Box 216
102 E. Johnson
Chelan, WA 98816
(509) 682-2022

Leavenworth Chamber of
Commerce
P.O. Box 327
703 U.S. Highway 2
Leavenworth, WA 98826
(509) 548-5807

Long Beach Peninsula Visitor's
Bureau
P.O. Box 562 (Long Beach
98631)
Highways 103 & 101
Seaview, WA 98644
(206) 642-2400

Lynden Chamber of Commerce
P.O. Box 647
1775 Front Street
Lynden, WA 98264
(206) 354-5995

Methow Valley Visitor Info.
Center
P.O. Box 665
Riverside Avenue & Bluff Street
Winthrop, WA 98862
(509) 996-2125 or (800) 551-
0111

Moses Lake Area Chamber of
Commerce
324 S. Pioneer Way
Moses Lake, WA 98837
(509) 765-7888

Newport Oldtown Chamber of
Commerce
P.O. Box 1795
Fourth & Washington Ave.
Newport, WA 99156
(509) 447-5812

Ocean Shores Chamber of
Commerce
P.O. Box 382
Catala Mall
Ocean Shroes, WA 98569
(206) 289-2451 or (800) 76-
BEACH

Olympia/Thurston County
Chamber of Commerce
1000 Plum Street
Olympia, WA 98501
(206) 357-3362

Omak Chamber of Commerce
Box 2087
401 Omak Avenue
Omak, WA 98841
(509) 826-1880

Oroville Chamber of Commerce
1728 Main Street
Oroville, WA 98844
(509) 476-2739

Pasco (Greater) Area Chamber
of Commerce
129 N. Third
Pasco, WA 99301
(509) 547-9755

Port Angeles Chamber of
Commerce
121 Railroad Avenue
Port Angeles, WA 98362
(206) 452-2363

Port Townsend Chamber of
Commerce
2437 Sims Way
Port Townsend, WA 98368
(206) 385-2722 or 385-2725

Pullman Chamber of
Commerce
N. 415 Grand Avenue
Pullman, WA 99163
(509) 334-3565

Republic Chamber of
Commerce
P.O. Box 1024
61 N. Kean Street
Republic, WA 99166
(509) 775-3387

Ritzville Chamber of Commerce
108 N. Adams
Ritzville, WA 99169
(509) 659-1547

San Juan County Chamber of
Commerce
P.O. Box 98
450 Spring Street
Friday Harbor, WA 98250

Seattle-King County
Visitors/Conv. Bureau
800 Convention Place
Seattle, WA 98101
(206) 461-5840

Sequim-Dungeness Valley
Chamber of Commerce
P.O. Box 907
1210 E. Washington
Sequim, WA 98382
(206) 683-6197

Shelton/Mason County
Chamber of Commerce
P.O. Box 666
Third & Railroad
Shelton, WA 98584

Skamania County Chamber of
Commerce
P.O. Box 1037
Second Street & Highway 14
Stevenson, WA 98648
(509) 427-8911

Snohomish Chamber of
Commerce
P.O. Box 135
116 Avenue B
Snohomish, WA 98290
(206) 568-2526

Snohomish County Visitor
Info. Center
1331 164th S.W.
Lynnwood, WA 98036
(206) 745-4133

Spokane Area Chamber of
Commerce
P.O. Box 2147
W. 1020 Riverside
Spokane, WA 99201
(509) 624-1393

Spokane Regional
Visitors/Conv. Bureau
W. 926 Sprague
Spokane, WA 99204
(509) 747-3230

Tacoma-Pierce County
Chamber of Commerce
P.O. Box 1933
950 Pacific Avenue
Tacoma, WA 98401
(206) 627-2175

Tri-Cities Visitors Bureau
P.O. Box 2241 (Tri-Cities
99302)
6951 Grandridge Blvd.
Kennewick, WA 99336
(509) 735-8486 or (800) 835-
0248

Twin Cities Chamber of
Commerce
P.O. Box 1263
National Avenue @ I-5
Chehalis, WA 98532

Twisp Information Center
P.O. Box 686
201 N. Methow Valley Highway
Twisp, WA 98856
(509) 997-2926

Vancouver/Clark County
Visitors/Conv. Bureau
1801 Interstate 5
Vancouver, WA 98663
(206) 696-1155

Walla Walla Area Chamber of
Commerce
P.O. Box 644
29 E. Sumach
Walla Walla, WA 99362
(509) 525-0850

Washington Coast Chamber of
Commerce
P.O. Box 430
State Highway 109 @ Ocean
City
Ocean Shores, WA 98569
(206) 289-4552

Wenatchee Chamber of
Commerce
P.O. Box 850
2 S. Chelan
Wenatchee, WA 98801
(509) 662-4774 or (800) 57-
APPLE (WA)

Westport/Grayland Chamber
of Commerce
P.O. Box 306
1200 N. Montesano
Westport, WA 98595
(206) 268-9422

Whatcom Chamber of
Commerce & Industry
P.O. Box 958
1203 Cornwall Avenue #102
Bellingham, WA 98225
(206) 734-1330

Woodland Tourist Info. Center
P.O. Box 1012
1225 Lewis River Drive
Woodland, WA 98674
(206) 225-9552

Yakima (Greater) Chamber of
Commerce
P.O. Box 1490
10 N. Ninth Street
Yakima, WA 98907
(509) 248-2021

Yakima Valley Visitors/Conv.
Bureau
10 N. Eighth Street
Yakima, WA 98901
(509) 575-1300

PHOTO CREDITS

INDEX

BOOKS ABOUT OREGON & WASHINGTON
by KiKi Canniff

A CAMPER'S GUIDE TO OREGON & WASHINGTON; A guide to the region's pay campgrounds. Perfect for campers who want showers, hookups or other civilized facilities. Opening material introduces the region's variety of terrains, climates, scenery and elevations. Each of the 1500 campground listings has complete details on facilities available plus easy to follow directions. *This handy guide belongs on every Northwest camper's 'must have' list."* **The Chronicle.** ($12.95)

FREE CAMPGROUNDS OF WASHINGTON & OREGON; Third Edition. This lightweight guide details the region's 700 free campgrounds. A terrific book for folks who enjoy camping close to nature. *"...very well done, easy to read and to understand ... the cost of this book is saved with the first campground used!"* **This Week Magazine.** ($8.95)

THE NORTHWEST GOLFER; A guide to the public golf courses in Washington & Oregon. Details the region's 252 public courses. Includes number of holes each course offers, total yardage, par, costs, rental information, what the terrain is like, type of hazards, facilities offered, directions, reservation information, and schedule. *"A HOLE IN ONE ... The whole information package about Northwest golf."* **The Oregonian.** ($9.95)

THE BEST FREE HISTORIC ATTRACTIONS IN OREGON & WASHINGTON. Includes the region's best ghost towns, covered bridges, aging lighthouses, museums, pioneer wagon trails, historic towns, archaeological digs, Indian artifact collections, railroad memorabilia, pioneer homes and more! *"KiKi Canniff is an expert on freebies"* **Woman's World Magazine.** ($10.95)

ABOUT THE AUTHOR

KiKi Canniff is a Portland writer who specializes in recreational attractions found in Oregon & Washington. She is an avid camper who enjoys hiking, golf, nature, history and exploring.

ORDER COUPON

Please send:

__BEST FREE HISTORIC ATTRACTIONS IN OR/WA;
Favorite Freebies Vol. 1 @ $10.95 ea. _____

__CAMPER'S GUIDE TO OR/WA @ $12.95 ea. _____

__FREE CAMPGROUNDS OF WA /OR @ $8.95 ea. _____

__ Camper's special - both guides $18.00/set _____

__THE NORTHWEST GOLFER @ $9.95 ea. _____

Shipping __2.00__

TOTAL ENCLOSED _____

Name _____

Address _____

City/State/Zip Code _____

Send this order coupon to Ki^2 Enterprises, P.O. Box 13322,
Portland, Oregon 97213

✂---✂

Please send:

__BEST FREE HISTORIC ATTRACTIONS IN OR/WA;
Favorite Freebies Vol. 1 @ $10.95 ea. _____

__CAMPER'S GUIDE TO OR/WA @ $12.95 ea. _____

__FREE CAMPGROUNDS OF WA /OR @ $8.95 ea. _____

_____Camper's special - both guides $18.00/set _____

__THE NORTHWEST GOLFER @ $9.95 ea. _____

Shipping __2.00__

TOTAL ENCLOSED _____

Name _____

Address _____

City/State/Zip Code _____

Send this order coupon to Ki^2 Enterprises, P.O. Box 13322,
Portland, Oregon 97213

COMING SOON:

**THE BEST FREE PLACES TO TAKE KIDS
IN OREGON & WASHINGTON**

**THE BEST FREE COASTAL ATTRACTIONS
IN OREGON & WASHINGTON**

**THE BEST FREE NATURAL & SCENIC
ATTRACTIONS IN OREGON & WASHINGTON**

To receive advance information on these and other books by KiKi Canniff send your name and address to Ki² Books, P.O. Box 13322, Portland, Oregon 97213.